Antrim & Derry
Edited by Mark Richardson

First published in Great Britain in 2008 by:
Young Writers
Remus House
Coltsfoot Drive
Peterborough
PE2 9JX
Telephone: 01733 890066
Website: www.youngwriters.co.uk

All Rights Reserved

© Copyright Contributors 2008

SB ISBN 978-1 84431 616 8

Foreword

Young Writers was established in 1991 and has been passionately devoted to the promotion of reading and writing in children and young adults ever since. The quest continues today. Young Writers remains as committed to the nurturing of poetic and literary talent as ever.

This year's Young Writers competition has proven as vibrant and dynamic as ever and we are delighted to present a showcase of the best poetry from across the UK and in some cases overseas. Each poem has been selected from a wealth of *Little Laureates 2008* entries before ultimately being published in this, our seventeenth primary school poetry series.

Once again, we have been supremely impressed by the overall quality of the entries we have received. The imagination, energy and creativity which has gone into each young writer's entry made choosing the poems a challenging and often difficult but ultimately hugely rewarding task - the general high standard of the work submitted ensured this opportunity to bring their poetry to a larger appreciative audience.

We sincerely hope you are pleased with this final collection and that you will enjoy *Little Laureates 2008 Antrim & Derry* for many years to come.

Contents

Anna Crowe (8) 1

Ballougry Primary School, Londonderry
Ethan Lapsley (10) 1
Tory Lapsley (10) 2
Andrew Porter (10) 3
Kathryn Marshall (10) 4

Carnaghts Primary School, Ballymena
Andrew Smyth (11) 4
Adam Gillen (11) 5
Neil McMaster (10) 5
Will Hutchison (10) 5
Emma McKay (11) 6
Rebecca Kennedy (11) 6
Daniel Jack Hogg (11) 6
Nicola Best (11) 7
Lauren McAuley (10) 7
Benjamin McIlroy (11) 7
Connor McDonald (11) 8
Kelly Turner (11) 8
Ciára Beattie (11) 8
Adam McBurney (11) 9

Drumahoe Primary School, Drumahoe
Stephanie McClay (10) 9
Demi Cragg (11) 9
Shannon Livingstone (11) 9
Adam Hewitt (11) 10
Jamie Anthony (11) 10
Ryan Marshall (11) 11
Gemma Lindsay (11) 11
Rodger Long (11) 12
Rachele Gordon (11) 12
Megan Stevenson (10) 13

Greystone Primary School, Antrim
  Dylan Wilson (7) — 13
  Bailey Davis (8) — 14

Kilmoyle Primary School, Ballymoney
  Abigail McIlhatton (11) — 14
  Scott Hickinson (10) — 15
  James Bleakly (11) — 15
  John McLaughlin (10) — 16
  Mark Young (10) — 16
  Emma Hartin (10) — 17
  Stacey Dunlop (11) — 17
  David Anderson (10) — 18
  Jeff Purdy (11) — 18
  Christopher Nevin (11) — 19
  Charlie Hayes (10) — 19
  Kathie Woodrow (10) — 20
  Rachel Grace Taggart (10) — 20
  Cameron Ashcroft (11) — 21
  Jamie-Lee Moore (10) — 21
  Justin McDonald (11) — 22
  Chloé Howard (10) — 22
  Alan Montgomery (10) — 23
  Andrew Millar (11) — 23
  Honor Elise Wilson (9) — 24
  Ruth Elizabeth Taggart (10) — 25
  Aimee Tawia (10) — 25
  Heather Clarke (10) — 26

Kilross Primary School, Magherafelt
  Claire McKinney (10) — 26
  Rebekah Sloss (11) — 27
  Andrew York (10) — 27
  James Thompson (10) — 27
  Zoë Campbell (11) — 28
  Jonathan Henderson (10) — 28
  James Parke (10) — 28
  James Marshall (10) — 29
  Ryan Brooks (11) — 29
  Sophie Moore (10) — 29
  Steven Hogg (10) — 30

Kirkinriola Primary School, Ballymena

Molly McCullough (9)	30
Harry Johnston (10)	30
Kate Walker (11)	31
Claire Herbison (11)	31
Alan Wallace (11)	32
Rachael Johnston (10)	32
Andrew Davison (10)	32
Emma Stewart (10)	33

Maghera Primary School, Maghera

Neil Richardson (8)	33
Kirsty Burnside (9)	33
Zara Nelson (8)	34
Malcolm Fry (10)	34
Rachel Lynch (9)	34
Reece Crawford (8)	35
Glen Crawford (9)	35
Hannah Leacock (9)	35
James Cunningham (9)	36
Rebecca Louise Johnston (10)	36
Anna Crawford (10)	36
Lauren Hilman (9)	37
Sam White (10)	37
Lee-Ann Bruce (9)	37
Rachel Miller (9)	38

Millquarter Primary School, Antrim

Cliodhna Gribbon (8)	38
Rachel McBride (8)	38
Dervla Bogner (8)	39
Lisa Walsh (7)	39
Orlaith Scullin (8)	39
Beverley Graffin (8)	40
Caolán McCloy (9)	40
Oisín Duffin (8)	41
Michael Martin (7)	41
Luke Paul Devlin (8)	41
Ciara Madden (7)	42
Shane O'Neill (8)	42
Eamon Kelly (7)	43

Aliesha McNally (8)	43
Patrick Magee (8)	43
Órlaith Prenter (7)	44

Newbuildings Primary School, Londonderry

Jack McClelland (9)	44
Amy Killen (9)	44
Alice McVeigh (8)	45
Gillian Dunn (9)	45
Hannah Thompson (9)	45
Mark Robinson (9)	46
Lewis Lecky (8)	46
Ross Thompson (9)	46
Justin McFaul (9)	47
Alex Warke (9)	47
Ross Dougherty (8)	47
Reece Sproule (9)	48
Hollie Wallace (9)	48
Nicole Rochester (9)	48
Brittany Craig (9)	49
James Philip McClelland (9)	49
James Nutt (8)	49
Charlie Johnston (9)	50

New Row Primary School, Castledawson

Niall Keenan (10)	50
Oisin Lennon (10)	50
Rian Connery (10)	51
Gareth Armstrong (11)	51
Pearse Loughran (10)	52
Cara O'Hagan (11)	52
Caoimhe McGoldrick (11)	53
Daniel O'Neill (11)	53
Daneka O'Hagan (11)	54
Emma McKeever (10)	54
Brigid McMullan (11)	55
Maria Doherty (10)	55
Niamh Bell (11)	56
Siobhan Burke (10)	56

Our Lady's Girls' Primary School, Belfast

Caitlin Huston (8)	57
Lauren Hamilton (8)	57
Emily Murphy (9)	57
Chantelle Markey (8)	58
Kaitlin Rock (9)	58
Rachael Anderson (8)	59
Monica Delaney (9)	59
Danielle Stewart (9)	60
Nicole Corbett (9)	60
Kirstyn Smith (9)	61
Fiona McGoran (9)	61
Morgan Kelly (9)	62
Rebecca McLaverty (9)	62
Emer Ward (8)	63
Sorcha McCarthy (10)	63
Seana Doran (11)	64
Amy McAnespie (11)	64
Clare McGibbon (10)	65
Niamh Scott (11)	65
Colleen Doherty (11)	66
Corrina Brady (11)	66
Melissa Keenan (10)	67
Una Kelly (10)	67
Hannah Cartmill (11)	68
Ciara Bradley (11)	68
Breanne McAuley (11)	69
Francesca Winters (10)	69
Rachel Cartmill (11)	70
Tory Henry (11)	70
Hannah Ferrin (11)	71
Nicole Service (11)	71
Eirinn Murphy (10)	72
Lauren Benson (10)	72
Cara McDonnell (7)	73
Enya Lawlor (10)	73
Meaghan Smyth (7)	73
Katie Burns (11)	74
Megan Dobbin (9)	74
Maureen Davidson (11)	75
Grace McCorry (10)	75

Sarah Marley (10)	76
Clodagh McIlkenny (10)	76
Courtney McIlkenny (9)	76
Grace McLaughlin (9)	77
Julie Donnelly (6)	77
Sophie Teer (7)	78
Emily McGearty (6)	78
Aimee McLarnon (7)	78
Amy-Jane Clarke (7)	79

Rosetta Primary School, Belfast

Nicole Amy Martin (10)	79
Nathan Quinn (11)	80
Rebecca Laverty (11)	80
Caitlin McNally (10)	81
Kyle Hurst (10)	81
John Lindsay (11)	82
Hazel Peacock (10)	82
Courtney Hewitt (11)	83
Yuki Mok (10)	83
Peter Foreman (11)	84
Adam Gribben (11)	84
Ryan Biggerstaff (11)	84
Megan Cotter (10)	85
Jordan McWilliams (11)	85

St Ciaran's Primary School, Cushendun

Patrick Quinn (11)	86
Rachael McNeill (11)	86
Anna McKay (11)	87
Eileen Magee (11)	87
Lauren McHugh (11)	88

St Mary's Primary School, Draperstown

Megan McKenna (10)	88
Una McCoy (10)	89
Dearbhla McCallion (8)	89
Dara Carlin (10)	90
Michael Donnelly (11)	90
Ben McCloskey (8)	91
Conor Dorrity (10)	91

Gemma Bradley (11)	92
Meghan McGillian (8)	92
Jon Paul Devlin (8)	93
Aine Michelle Lagan (10)	93
Rory McGuigan (8)	93
Cathy McKenna (11)	94
Aaron McCloskey (8)	94
Carla McGuigan (7)	94
Ellen Kelly (11)	95
Aine Gray (8)	95
Cara McGoldrick (8)	95
Dermot Hegarty (10)	96
Annie McEldowney (10)	96
Thomas Gillespie (11)	97
Rachel Kelly (11)	97
Caroline Rafferty (10)	98
Cahir McEldowney (11)	98
Fionnuala Hegarty (11)	99
Stephen Halferty (11)	99
Damien McCoy (8)	100
Clare Cuskeran (10)	101
Adam Harlow (11)	101
Ciaran Breen (10)	102

St Michael's Primary School, Belfast

Elena Torres (11)	102
Clodagh Smith (11)	103
Niall Smyth (10)	103
Dermot O'Hare (11)	104
Joanne Madden-McKee (10)	104
Niamh Kelly (10)	105
Jacob Meehan (11)	105
Nicholas Kearney (10)	106
Becky Guirova (11)	106
Niamh Healy (10)	107
Catherine Kilgallen (11)	107
Ben O'Kane (8)	108
Cormac Meehan (11)	108
Fiona Currie (8)	109
Amy Gogarty (9)	109
Tom McVeigh (9)	110

Brandon Daly (11)	110
Aobh Hughes (8)	111
Daire Magee (8)	111
Declan McCartney (9)	112
Dáire Cumiskey (10)	112
Sean McGrillen (11)	112
Alex Symes (9)	113
Jake Carlin (9)	113
Francesca McVey (11)	113
Timothy Cunningham (8)	114
Olivia Ray (9)	114
Tara Faulkner (9)	114
Andy Harney (8)	115
Tony Crawford (9)	115
Keela McConville (9)	115
Hannah Griffin (9)	116
Laura Jane Quinn (8)	116
Lorcan Fahy (8)	116

St Paul's Primary School, Londonderry

Ciara O'Doherty (8)	117
Reece Ogle (9)	117
Bradley Belgrave (8)	117
Caitlin Goodfellow (8)	118
Sean Burke	118
Tony Whoriskey (8)	118
Feargal Mellon	119
Christopher McQuaid (8)	119
Shay Cavanagh (8)	119
Samantha Boyle (11)	120
Odhran Scarlett (10)	120
Bronagh Robinson (10)	121
Gary James Burke (10)	121
Shauneen Cavanagh (10)	122
Priscilla Corcoran (9)	122
Chloé McClintock (10)	123
Jamie Dunne (10)	123
Demilee Collett (10)	124
Reece O'Kane (8)	124
Caolán Ramsay (10)	125

Saoirse McCormick (10)   125
Aaron Dalzell (10)   126

Woodlawn Primary School, Carrickfergus
Shannon Gaw (9)   126
Victoria Shearer (10)   127
Courtney Best (9)   127
Rebekah Stewart (8)   127
Erin McAllister (10)   128
Leah Thompson (10)   128
Simon Scott (10)   129
Jamie Karl Wallace (10)   129
Emma Baird (10)   130
Chloe Greenaway (10)   130
Caitlin Eve Robin (9)   131
Ashleigh Milliken (9)   131
Demi Davies (10)   132
Hannah Barbour (10)   132
Sophie Duff (10)   132
Abigail Kerr (10)   133
Sophie Irwin (11)   133
Abby Nicholl (10)   133
Chloe Mitchell (11)   134
Nicole Magill (10)   134
Ben Grange (11)   134
Lee Beattie (11)   135
Ryan Dillon (11)   135
Jordan Bell (11)   135
Emily Brownlee (11)   136
Rachel Close (11)   136
Chealsea Waite (11)   136
Jake Adams (11)   137
Ellen Minford (11)   137
Shannon Clarke (11)   137
Reece McDowell (11)   138
Jessica McCully (11)   138
Leigh-Anne Gould (11)   138
Laura Smyth (10)   139
Rebecca Adams (11)   139
Reece Griffith (10)   139
Rebecca McIlwaine (7)   140

Ben Crook (7)   140
Amber Eyres (10)   140
Adam Crook (8)   141
Katie Mitchell (8)   141

The Poems

Ducks

Ducks quack
Anywhere,
At any animal,
At any place,
While children play,
While adults run,
At seals coughing,
At bears growling,
They don't care,
Ducks quack,
Anywhere.

Anna Crowe (8)

What Is He?

My pet cannot go out to play
Or sell his house or rent it;
But when he moves,
His house moves too
And nothing can prevent it.

When he moves, it's not too fast,
In fact, it's sometimes rather boring,
But when I try to sleep at night,
I can't because he's snoring.

His diet's very healthy,
No chips or chocolate there,
But as long as we have dandelions,
Young Bruce will not despair!

Can you guess what my pet is?
He's a tropical bloke
And that's no joke,
He's a
Cherry head red foot tortoise.

Ethan Lapsley (10)
Ballougry Primary School, Londonderry

Skiing!

I went skiing over New Year,
Schoolwork was happily nowhere near,
We were off to Austria where it's cool,
In our hotel there was a lovely pool.

I was up in the morning at half-past eight,
The skis we had to carry were such a weight,
Up in the chairlift we went to the top,
If you looked down, it was such a huge drop!

We skied for two hours,
In the snowy showers,
We skied down the mountain really fast
And as always, Mummy was last!

Black runs, red runs, we did them all,
Although I admit, on one I did fall!
Our instructor, who's name was Fred,
Made us ski till time for bed!

Home to our hotel in time for dinner,
Everyone felt a little thinner!
New Year's Eve was brilliant there,
Fireworks going off everywhere!

Günter was our barman's name,
He must have thought we were insane!
We had a waiter named Marcel,
What he said, I cannot tell!

The week had gone, we had to go,
About my holiday, you now know!

Tory Lapsley (10)
Ballougry Primary School, Londonderry

My Family

My family is very strange
I thought you'd like to know
Me, my sister and my dad
And my mum make such a show!

My baby sister, Rachel
She's quite a laugh machine
She lay down on my lap
And tried to eat my jeans!

And then, of course, there's Dad
The dumbest of them all
I came in through the front door
He said, 'Hello there, Paul!'

My mum, she's really mad
She's always very cross
She runs about the house
Screaming that she's the boss.

Obviously there's me
The coolest that there is
I sometimes dream about Fanta
I even taste the fizz!

I'm soon going to turn eleven
That'll turn me round the bend
But now I think it's time to say
It's finally the end!

Andrew Porter (10)
Ballougry Primary School, Londonderry

Harry Potter

The Harry Potter series are my favourite books
They're much more exciting than they look
On my table, there they lie
When I read, the imagination flies.
Year one - Quirrel's life he did take
Year two - he killed a giant snake
Year three - Dementors he did fight
Year four - Voldemort returned at dead of night
Year five - he struggled for his mind
Year six - pain and suffering he did find
Year seven - I'm not going to tell
You want the reason? Oh, very well!
If I tell you, you won't read the book
Which is a pity, because you really should look.
The books can take you by surprise
Leave you wandering with big wide eyes
Your mind will twist, jump and bend
Long before you reach the end.

Kathryn Marshall (10)
Ballougry Primary School, Londonderry

Eels

Slimy things
Moving, slithery, slimy
Very ugly creatures
Disgusting!

Andrew Smyth (11)
Carnaghts Primary School, Ballymena

Boardslide

It happened yesterday,
I managed to land 0boardslide,
My worst fear was that my board would snap!
Now I can land a boardslide,
My board won't snap if I do it right.

Adam Gillen (11)
Carnaghts Primary School, Ballymena

Spaghetti

Spaghetti
Messy, spicy
Slurping, sliding, falling
Between my plate and mouth
Delicious.

Neil McMaster (10)
Carnaghts Primary School, Ballymena

Flight To America

Over the summer,
I went over to the USA,
I was scared the plane would crash,
The plane didn't crash,
Don't always expect the worst in life.

Will Hutchison (10)
Carnaghts Primary School, Ballymena

Family

F amily is a close-knit bond
A lways there for me
M any times we laugh and cry
I t is great to be part of a family
L ove is shared amongst us
Y ou too can be part of a family, love and patience is all it takes.

Emma McKay (11)
Carnaghts Primary School, Ballymena

What Path Will I Take?

What path will I take?
What path is right?
What path will lead me to the right place?
What path is the safest?
What path is the most beautiful?

Rebecca Kennedy (11)
Carnaghts Primary School, Ballymena

Football

F ernando Torres plays for Liverpool
O wn goals are very embarrassing
O h, it helps to shoot the right way
T oure plays for Arsenal
B all is very nice
A lonso plays for Liverpool
L ots of people like it
L ots of people play it.

Daniel Jack Hogg (11)
Carnaghts Primary School, Ballymena

Life

L ife is like love
I t is everlasting
F orever and eternal
E very day of our lives.

Nicola Best (11)
Carnaghts Primary School, Ballymena

A Spade - Kennings

Sand builder
Soil breaker
Cement mixer
Earth filler
Hole digger
Flower planter
Castle maker
Stone picker.

Lauren McAuley (10)
Carnaghts Primary School, Ballymena

Rugby

R ugby is a rough game
U nexpected tackles may come
G allop along to score a try
B e very quick or they might catch you
Y ell for joy when the conversion is kicked.

Benjamin McIlroy (11)
Carnaghts Primary School, Ballymena

Rugby

R ough tackles
U nsensible
G ood when Six Nations was won by England
B ad sport if under five
Y ell when England win!

Connor McDonald (11)
Carnaghts Primary School, Ballymena

Teachers

The teachers at my school,
They think I'm such a fool,
I think of myself as very smart,
Even though I can't cut a fraction in part,
But teachers, are they really so smart?

Kelly Turner (11)
Carnaghts Primary School, Ballymena

Carnaghts

C aring for others
A ssembly - we pray to God
R unning to keep us fit and healthy
N o worries at all
A lways a teacher to talk to
G ardening skills in the backyard
H appy and cheerful children
T eachers always listen
S chool is a special place for me.

Ciára Beattie (11)
Carnaghts Primary School, Ballymena

Rugby

R uck ball on the ground
U nder the arm should be the ball
G rab the ball out of the mud
B rilliant friends make brilliant teams
Y ou're the one who can make the difference in the team.

Adam McBurney (11)
Carnaghts Primary School, Ballymena

Haiku Poem

Stephanie's my name
I live at 15 Elm Park
And I have a dog.

Stephanie McClay (10)
Drumahoe Primary School, Drumahoe

Haiku Poem

My name is Demi,
I live at 15 Elm Park
I have a goldfish.

Demi Cragg (11)
Drumahoe Primary School, Drumahoe

Haiku

Pets are lovely things
And I love my pet kitten
And she is so cute.

Shannon Livingstone (11)
Drumahoe Primary School, Drumahoe

Haiku Poems

I have an uncle
Who has a dog and a fish
The dog's called Rocket

I went to Blackpool
It was sunny all the time
I had a great time

What I like doing
I like playing with my friends
Even when it's wet.

Adam Hewitt (11)
Drumahoe Primary School, Drumahoe

Haiku Poems

My mum is the best
But not as good as my dad
He gives me money

Football is my game
Scoring great goals is my aim
I'd like to find fame

Winter's nearly done
Ready for the summer sun
Get your sunblock out.

Jamie Anthony (11)
Drumahoe Primary School, Drumahoe

Haiku Poems

I hate school a lot
Especially the teachers
I hate the work too

There are four seasons
My favourite is summer
Some like winter too

I went to Sweden
I thought it was brilliant
My mum thought so too.

Ryan Marshall (11)
Drumahoe Primary School, Drumahoe

Haiku Poems

Friends, the very best
They always look out for you
Friends are forever

There are four seasons
In a year, winter and spring
Summer and autumn

Pets are animals
That need looking after, pets
Need to be loved too.

Gemma Lindsay (11)
Drumahoe Primary School, Drumahoe

Haiku Poems

I like Wayne Rooney
He is a great footballer
He is a striker

Rugby is my sport
It is very aggressive
It is very fun

Gortatole we went
Our class really enjoyed it
It was mostly wet.

Rodger Long (11)
Drumahoe Primary School, Drumahoe

Haiku Poems

A chocolate Aero
It fills my mouth with sweetness
Oh, how delicious

My granda's hobby
Is to sit and watch the birds
In his back garden

The fours seasons are
Spring, summer, autumn, winter
Cold and also warm.

Rachele Gordon (11)
Drumahoe Primary School, Drumahoe

Haikus

I went to Cyprus
For my holiday last year
It was really fun

Hillary Duff is
A singer and an actress
I think she is good

I have a pet dog
Her name is Daisy and she
Is really playful.

Megan Stevenson (10)
Drumahoe Primary School, Drumahoe

In The Sun

Going to the airport can be such stress,
Packing luggage, everywhere is a mess,
Holidays are fun, we can't wait to go,
Having fun in the sun, away from the ice and snow.

When we arrived there, we had a cup of tea,
Then we went down to see the sea,
At the beach we built a sandcastle,
Which was a great deal of hassle.

Our holidays are over, it's time to go,
Back to the ice and snow,
We had a good time, so we can't complain,
I think we'll go on holidays again.

Dylan Wilson (7)
Greystone Primary School, Antrim

The Mermaid

A mermaid sat
On a sandy rock
And her eyes gleamed, soft and green,
'Come with me,' she called
'And I'll take you away
To the land beneath the sea.
We'll ride on a dolphin,
We'll tickle a whale,
Eat seaweed cake for our tea'
And she held out her hand,
As she dived through the waves,
'Come with me,
    Come with me,
        Come with me.'

Bailey Davis (8)
Greystone Primary School, Antrim

Mount Vesuvius

Doing what we always do every day,
Housework, cooking and cleaning.
Suddenly, a loud crashing sound
Can be heard miles away.
Vesuvius has blown its top,
River of lava come pouring out,
Clouds of ash go around in the air.

People running and screaming everywhere,
Trying to protect themselves.
Hot ash raining down on them,
Fiery rocks come crashing out,
Poison drifts around in the air.

The little town is now in pieces,
People come to see their houses,
Lying in piles of dust and dirt.
Everything has turned to stone,
The little town is now still and silent.

Abigail McIlhatton (11)
Kilmoyle Primary School, Ballymoney

I See You Eagle, Soaring Through The Air

Flying around, eating small animals
With your hooked beak
Eagle, I see you soaring through the air
Eagle, your strong legs and feet
Eagle, I see you soaring through the air
At such great speed
Eagle, I see you soaring through the air
With great agility
I see you eagle, soaring through the air
With big, swift wings
I see you eagle, soaring through the air.

Scott Hickinson (10)
Kilmoyle Primary School, Ballymoney

Mount Vesuvius

It was still and quiet
Mount Vesuvius looking fierce
But doing nothing
Then it happened . . .
Mount Vesuvius erupted
Bang! The lava burst out
The rocks flew everywhere.

People running and coughing
The sight was terrifying
You could hear screams
The lava got closer and closer
Some people stayed in their houses
The lava had come
Everyone was praying to their gods.

People were dying
They were melting in the lava
People were sweating with the heat
None of them survived
That was the story
Of great Mount Vesuvius.

James Bleakly (11)
Kilmoyle Primary School, Ballymoney

Computer

Computer
I see you

Computer
I see you
Alone

Computer
I hear your
Fan

Computer
I shall use
You

Computer
I learn from
You

Computer I will
Turn you
Off.

John McLaughlin (10)
Kilmoyle Primary School, Ballymoney

Snow Leopard

Stalking stealthily in the snow
I see you snow leopard
Watching a deer
Waiting for the right moment
Striking so swiftly
Running at such fast speeds
Catching it so strongly
Dragging it away in the snow
Eating so proudly
Not many of you around anymore
Not aware of what danger you are in
Snow leopard, the most majestic of animals.

Mark Young (10)
Kilmoyle Primary School, Ballymoney

Mallard

In the deep blue water, mallard,
I saw you swimming.

Your flat, orange beak, mallard,
Looking for food.

In the deep blue water, mallard,
I saw you swimming.

Your short, orange legs, mallard
And your tiny, webbed feet.

In the deep blue water, mallard,
I saw you swimming.

Bright green, brown, black and white, mallard,
Your neat feathers glistening.

In the deep blue water, mallard,
I saw you swimming.

Emma Hartin (10)
Kilmoyle Primary School, Ballymoney

Mount Vesuvius

Sitting there in the street
Calm and quiet
When suddenly there was a rumble,
The top of Mount Vesuvius had blown its top
The roaring, booming sounds of it,
The sounds were horrible.

Children holding their ears,
People screaming,
Children were coughing.

When the volcano stopped,
The sizzling lava stopped
All the people were delighted
And there's Mount Vesuvius,
Sitting there like before.

Stacey Dunlop (11)
Kilmoyle Primary School, Ballymoney

Arsenal

Five Arsenal players
In the changing room
If you put a pin in the ball
It will go *boom!*

Four Arsenal players
Standing on the pitch
Eight-nil up
Their opponents are in a ditch.

Three Arsenal players
Give the keeper a nightmare
Eduardo rockets it
The nets have a tear.

Two Arsenal players
Scoring non-stop
When Eduardo blasts it
There is a deafening *pop!*

One Arsenal player
Standing on his own
He is scoring everywhere
You would think there was a clone.

David Anderson (10)
Kilmoyle Primary School, Ballymoney

Eduardo

From a distance I see Eduardo
Running quickly
Ugly tackling
Shooting brilliantly
Wonderfully scoring
People think he's excellent
He feels he's the
Best in the world.

Jeff Purdy (11)
Kilmoyle Primary School, Ballymoney

Big, Old Vesuvius

Lying in Italy
With nothing to do
Decided to blow his top
On little Pompeii

At first it roared
Ash appeared
People running
Unable to escape its rage

People choking
Coughing because of the ash
Poison consuming their lungs
There was no way back

The sky was black
The air was thick
They would die at any moment
Because of this fearful monster

Once he had finished
The victor stood proud
He was done with Pompeii
Then he thought
Wait for my next explosion!

Christopher Nevin (11)
Kilmoyle Primary School, Ballymoney

Frank Lampard

From a distance
I see Frank Lampard
Hitting powerfully
Quickly running
Mostly scoring
Striking accurately
People adore him
Because he is the best
And he knows it!

Charlie Hayes (10)
Kilmoyle Primary School, Ballymoney

Mount Vesuvius

Mount Vesuvius is a volcano
A very famous one too
When it exploded in 1944
It was a very big boom

People running, screaming everywhere
Not knowing what to do
Sizzling lava running down
Masses of ash flying upwards

Worried faces
Running to the gate
Everyone pushing, trying to get out
And escape the drifting poison

Some didn't want to leave their homes
A very big mistake they did make
Some lay in bed
And some stood in the doorway

Then the lava ran over them
Killing them and covering them
Raining down on them
Was the rock of Mount Vesuvius.

Kathie Woodrow (10)
Kilmoyle Primary School, Ballymoney

I Like Chocolate

I like chocolate
The soft, melting, caramel kind.
The make-it-into-chocolate-bunnies kind
Caramel dripping down your chin.
Eating and munching
I do like chocolate!

Rachel Grace Taggart (10)
Kilmoyle Primary School, Ballymoney

Mount Vesuvius

Sitting so quietly
No one knows
Suddenly *bang! boom!*
It blows its top off
Rivers of lava
Ash everywhere
Hot, red, sizzling lava
Clouds of smoke
Masses of ash
Unstoppable
Molten lava
Everything stops
Not a house in sight
Quiet again
No people
Oh, big, old Mount Vesuvius.

Cameron Ashcroft (11)
Kilmoyle Primary School, Ballymoney

Mount Vesuvius

Mount Vesuvius
Quiet and peaceful
Until rumbling
People screaming
Clouds of smoke shooting out.

It was a loud explosion
Lava running everywhere
The earth was shaking
And everyone ran to their homes
And many people died.

Jamie-Lee Moore (10)
Kilmoyle Primary School, Ballymoney

Eagle

In the light blue sky
Eagle
I see you fly.

Swooping down
To get your prey.

In the light blue sky
Eagle
I see you fly.

With your long, sharp talons
And your little, short legs.

In the light blue sky
Eagle
I see you fly.

With beautiful black and white feathers
And wide, stretchy wings.

In the light blue sky
Eagle
I see you fly.

Justin McDonald (11)
Kilmoyle Primary School, Ballymoney

I Like Doctor Who

I like Doctor Who
The scary, exciting, dangerous kind
The scare-your-pants-off kind
The hide behind the sofa
The monsters going to jump out
I do like Doctor Who!

Chloé Howard (10)
Kilmoyle Primary School, Ballymoney

Mount Vesuvius

Vesuvius, the still enormous volcano
Then suddenly, *boom!*
It blows off its top
Crash!
Fiery rocks come hurling out
Bursting lava
And ear-piercing rumbles

Men, women and children
Screaming, shouting and sprinting
Falling rocks setting fire to the town
Run, run, faster and faster
Vesuvius the massive
Serial killer
Poison and fire
Have taken their toll.

Alan Montgomery (10)
Kilmoyle Primary School, Ballymoney

Anelka

I watch Anelka
Scoring amazingly
Gently dribbling
Attacking brilliantly
Powerfully kicking
The coolest scorer ever!

Andrew Millar (11)
Kilmoyle Primary School, Ballymoney

Victory For Vesuvius

Mount Vesuvius, as peaceful as can be
But that is not the way it was in 79AD
Vesuvius, the victor, Vesuvius the grand
Definitely the volcano known throughout the land.

Vesuvius has blown his top
He's raging, as cross as can be!
Help, he's chucking rocks at me!
With a *boom* and a *bash,* a *roar* and a *crash*
Vesuvius explodes!

Rivers of lava chasing the people
Catching them in its grasp
Hundreds of people running away
From the terror in Italy
Rocks are flying
And children are crying.

Red, fiery,
Burning, blazing,
Dangerous,
It will frazzle
It will scorch
It's . . .
Vesuvius!

It's burned and buried in Herculaneum
Flamed and sizzled in Pompeii
It's burnt a lot
We've learnt a lot
About Vesuvius today.

Honor Elise Wilson (9)
Kilmoyle Primary School, Ballymoney

Mount Vesuvius

Mount Vesuvius just sitting
With nothing else to do,
But suddenly, there comes a sound
That will scare and frighten you!

It will *boom* and *bash*
It will *roar* and *crash,*
Everyone in Italy will run
Until the erupting volcano is done.

When the lava comes pouring down
There will be worries and frowns,
Lots of clouds of smoke
This is just a joke!

People are running away
From the disaster in Italy,
Pompeii is buried and burnt
Now we have learnt
About *Mount Vesuvius!*

Ruth Elizabeth Taggart (10)
Kilmoyle Primary School, Ballymoney

The Baby Owl

In the tall, brown tree, I see an owl
Wisely waiting for its food to arrive
Squawking with its mouth wide open
Hoping for a nice, juicy worm
Then, in comes its mother
Swooping down with her long, graceful wings
The chick feels happy to be fed
Then off to sleep in its lovely feather bed.

Aimee Tawia (10)
Kilmoyle Primary School, Ballymoney

Dolphin

Dolphin, I see you
In the clear blue water

Dolphin, I see you
Swimming

Dolphin, I see you
Eating lots of fish

Dolphin, I see you
Jumping in the air

I like you, dolphin
Dolphin is very happy.

Heather Clarke (10)
Kilmoyle Primary School, Ballymoney

Anger

Anger, anger
It smells like smoke in your eyes
It is a roaring lion
Red, hot, fiery.

It feels like someone
Spitting at you
It looks like a volcano exploding!
It tastes like rotten potatoes.

Anger, anger
I detest anger!
It reminds me of Brussels sprouts!

Claire McKinney (10)
Kilross Primary School, Magherafelt

Sadness

Sadness is tears streaming down your face
It is as black as night
Sadness is my pony dying
It is a rainy day
Sadness is a cold, dark day
Sadness is no one understanding me
Sadness is Jesus on the cross.

Rebekah Sloss (11)
Kilross Primary School, Magherafelt

Anger

Anger is a bomb that soon is going to blast off
Anger reminds me of a burning fire
Anger sounds like a volcano erupting
Anger tastes like a red-hot chilli
Anger smells like the lava from a volcano
Anger looks like noisy fireworks exploding in the sky
Anger feels like a bull ready to charge.

Andrew York (10)
Kilross Primary School, Magherafelt

Anger

Anger looks like something red
Like an exploding fire on Bonfire Night
Anger is like a bull racing through the fields
Anger feels like Hell
Anger boils up inside me until I could explode!
Anger makes me mad!
Anger reminds me of a half-eaten dead fox
Anger is a roaring red quad racing past
Anger is Mummy shouting at me!

James Thompson (10)
Kilross Primary School, Magherafelt

Laughter

Laughter is lovely, twinkly music
Which goes around the world
It's as sweet as cake
Like a purring kitten
But best of all, it tickles your belly
Which makes you giggle
Laughter smells like honey
And is like a shiny, scented flower
But most of all, it reminds me
Of my friends having fun together.

Zoë Campbell (11)
Kilross Primary School, Magherafelt

Anger

Anger is red as red as a fire
Anger feels like you are a volcano about to explode
It tastes like something very hot in your mouth
Anger looks like a blazing fire
It smells like smoke
Anger is someone about to hit an enemy.

Jonathan Henderson (10)
Kilross Primary School, Magherafelt

Laughter

Laughter sounds like a purring cat with a microphone
It reminds me of my mum singing out of tune
It looks like a circus clown
And tastes like sweet, sweet honey
It smells like a peaceful town
Laughter makes you pink, especially when you get money
Laughter is a joke
To control it, you would need a yoke!

James Parke (10)
Kilross Primary School, Magherafelt

Laughter

Laughter tastes like Red Bull
It reminds me of tricks and jokes
It sounds like something funny
Laughter smells like honey
Laughter is the colour pink
Laughter is like a clown
A clown with funny clothes
And a huge red nose.

James Marshall (10)
Kilross Primary School, Magherafelt

Laughter

Laugher looks like a funny clown
And smells like ice cream
It sounds like funny poems
And tastes like candy
Laughter is pink
It reminds me of tickles and jokes.

Ryan Brooks (11)
Kilross Primary School, Magherafelt

Silence

S ilence
I s golden
L ike the sun
E ven silence has a scent
N ever heard
C omes every so often
E verything has silence sometimes.

Sophie Moore (10)
Kilross Primary School, Magherafelt

Anger

Anger feels like a hard rock hitting me in the stomach
It looks like a burning fire
It sounds like a roaring lion
Anger reminds me of murder
It tastes like a rotten egg
Anger smells like smoke up my nose
It is red and fiery
Anger is a pit bull terrier.

Steven Hogg (10)
Kilross Primary School, Magherafelt

My Friends

My friends mean a lot to me,
They have always been there for me,
I can trust them with everything,
They give me laughter, kindness,
Happiness and most of all,
Friendship,
Nothing means more to me
Than my four best friends.

Molly McCullough (9)
Kirkinriola Primary School, Ballymena

Rugby

R ough, reckless and dirty I play
U nlucky if the other team scores a try
G ood, we win, we win
B rilliant - we are at the top of the league
Y ou are the losers and we are the winners!

Harry Johnston (10)
Kirkinriola Primary School, Ballymena

My Favourite Author!

I wonder if there's an author,
One you really like,
Maybe it's J K Rowling,
Or even Debbie White.

If you're like me,
You'll make the right choice
And pick J K Rowling,
She drives in a Rolls Royce,
Or maybe even a Jag,
Both worth one million
And not be one bit sad!

Kate Walker (11)
Kirkinriola Primary School, Ballymena

I Swear I Saw A Fairy

I swear I saw a fairy,
I did, I did, I did,
She was sitting on the doghouse,
Fixing her tiny pink shoe,
She flew about the garden,
Smelling all the pretty flowers,
She flew next to the rose bush
And caught her sparkly pink dress on a thorn,
I ran out the door to feel the warm summer's day,
I walked towards her and unhooked her dress,
Then she spoke, her voice was tiny,
But I could make out what she said,
She flew away, towards the sky,
So, now I look out of the window,
To look for that little fairy.

Claire Herbison (11)
Kirkinriola Primary School, Ballymena

Massey Ferguson

M y uncle was voted the best at fixing Massey Ferguson in Northern Ireland
A Massey is the best
S teering is the best
S till Massey is the best
E veryone likes Masseys
Y ards will never get dirty with Massey Ferguson.

Alan Wallace (11)
Kirkinriola Primary School, Ballymena

Dogs

Some dogs are fluffy little creatures
And they come with lots of features,
Nose and ears, mouth and tail,
Their puppy dog eyes could never fail.

Other dogs may be fierce and bad,
When they see strangers, they go mad,
These big dogs may start a fight
And if they want, they might just bite!

Rachael Johnston (10)
Kirkinriola Primary School, Ballymena

Tractors

T ractors are super!
R ed Massey Ferguson trundles down the rough lane
A cco harvester awaits in the golden field
C rops coming down and through the harvester they go
T ractor pulls along side it and out they come in huge amounts
O ut of the field and into the silo
R etire for the day in the nice, warm barn
S ilent in bed, the scruffy old farmer goes to sleep.

Andrew Davison (10)
Kirkinriola Primary School, Ballymena

The Jungle

The jungle is lovely and warm,
The jungle is like a wild farm
And on the ground I see a green snake,
I wonder what shape the flower will make?
Up above, I see a monkey,
Climbing on a tree that looks very wonky,
Although the jungle is warm, it is also wet,
The Amazon is where the jungle is set,
I saw a forest fire with a non-stop burn,
I have to go, but with hope, I'll return!

Emma Stewart (10)
Kirkinriola Primary School, Ballymena

How To Make A Budgie

Feathers like a fluffy coat,
Head like a small dome,
Claws like a sharp knife,
His body is like a fluffy egg,
His legs are like two thin sticks,
His beak is like a dark yellow banana.

Neil Richardson (8)
Maghera Primary School, Maghera

How To Make A Dog

You need . . .
Tail like a curly fry,
Ears like a fluffy leaf,
Body like an oval,
Nose as black as coal,
Head like a fluffy football,
Paws as big as my hands.

Kirsty Burnside (9)
Maghera Primary School, Maghera

How To Make A Kitten

You need . . .
A head like a round ball,
Whiskers like a long bit of string,
A tail like a long worm,
Fur like a soft bed,
Eyes like sparkly water,
Body like a long hand,
Ears like a pointy carrot.

Zara Nelson (8)
Maghera Primary School, Maghera

How To Make A Dog

It needs . . .
Fur like a pillow,
Ears like a flopping, waving hand,
Teeth like small knives,
A tail like a tree stump,
Head like a pear,
A body like a ball of fur.

Malcolm Fry (10)
Maghera Primary School, Maghera

How To Make A Dog

You need . . .
Eyes like shining stars,
Body like a ball of fluff,
Ears like a leaf,
Nose like moist leather,
Paws, big and small,
Tail as fluffy as a duster,
Teeth as small as a pencil lead,
A head as round as a teddy.

Rachel Lynch (9)
Maghera Primary School, Maghera

How To Make A Rhino

You need . . .
A horn like a sharp dagger,
Skin as hard as a big rock,
A tail like a dog's with a ball of wool at the end,
Feet as big as elephant feet,
A body, big like an elephant's
And eyes as angry as a lion's.

Reece Crawford (8)
Maghera Primary School, Maghera

How To Make A Dog

You need . . .
Ears like floppy waves,
Tail as wide as a tree stump,
Feet as long as knives,
A body like a ball of waves,
Claws like a sharp knife.

Glen Crawford (9)
Maghera Primary School, Maghera

How To Make A Puppy

You need . . .
Paws like a rough stone,
Teeth like knives,
Legs like a thick book,
Ears as sensitive as a glass ball,
A nose as wet as a swimming pool,
A body like a wheel,
A head like a hard football,
Hair as soft as a fluffy pillow,
Claws as pointy as a witch's hat,
A tail as long as a chip.

Hannah Leacock (9)
Maghera Primary School, Maghera

How To Make A Dolphin

It needs . . .
A snout like a skyscraper's top,
Flippers like a fanning fan
And eyes like black beads,
Tail swerves like the underwater current
And a body, rubbery like an elastic band.

James Cunningham (9)
Maghera Primary School, Maghera

How To Make A Pig!

She needs . . .
A tail like curly fries or a spring,
Body colour, soft and pink, like a newborn baby's skin,
A snout like a snuffly, powerful hoover,
Her trotters so small, they can hardly be seen,
Legs like small tree stumps,
Ears like a yummy, triangular piece of pizza,
Eyes like the beautiful midnight sky!

Rebecca Louise Johnston (10)
Maghera Primary School, Maghera

How To Make An Owl

He needs . . .
Wings as long as a bus and as silent as a mouse,
Eyes as sharp as a thousand knives,
A beak as strong as a dragon!
Claws as scary as a bear,
Feathers as mighty as a knight in shining armour!
Head as round as a dome
And a body as long and slender as a snake!

Anna Crawford (10)
Maghera Primary School, Maghera

How To Make A French Lop

It needs . . .
A body like a long, furry egg,
Fur like a soft and cuddly bed,
Ears as floppy as a soft piece of paper,
A tail too tiny to see,
Claws as sharp as knives
And feet as big as hands.

Lauren Hilman (9)
Maghera Primary School, Maghera

How To Make A Komodo Dragon

It needs . . .
Sharp claws like a raptor's,
Scales like hard rock,
Tail like thick lead,
Tongue like forked knives,
Teeth like strong steel,
Saliva like deadly acid.

Sam White (10)
Maghera Primary School, Maghera

How To Make A Cat!

You need . . .
Ears like a triangle,
Body like a potato,
Tail like a fluffy snake
Round, green eyes like jewels.

Lee-Ann Bruce (9)
Maghera Primary School, Maghera

How To Make A Donkey

It needs . . .
Ears like a carrot with a round top,
Eyes like small golf balls,
Legs like thick, bent sticks,
Tail like a long, fluffy pencil case
And a nose as soft as velvet.

Rachel Miller (9)
Maghera Primary School, Maghera

My Dog

My dog's name
Is Shadow
She is three years old
She has green eyes
And floppy ears
And a very short tail.

Cliodhna Gribbon (8)
Millquarter Primary School, Antrim

My Cat

I have a cat called Figo, he's a boy
I love him, he is funny
He plays with my tie
He's hungry all the time
He catches mice
And he thinks they are nice
He plays with them in the garden
He is white and brown.

Rachel McBride (8)
Millquarter Primary School, Antrim

Pets

I love Smokey my rabbit
He is grey and fluffy
He sits around all day
And sometimes eats hay
He's got big brown eyes
And a little pink nose
That he twitches from time to time.

Dervla Bogner (8)
Millquarter Primary School, Antrim

My Sisters

They always scream and shout at me
They call me names and pull my hair
They lock me in our playhouse
Take my turn, but they don't care
My sisters!

They share their toys and sweets with me
Comfort me when I fall
They cuddle up when we watch TV
And they think I'm best of all!
My sisters!

Lisa Walsh (7)
Millquarter Primary School, Antrim

My Pets

I think that my pets are very nice
I hate to say that they are mice
They run around along the floor
And keep on climbing up the door!

Orlaith Scullin (8)
Millquarter Primary School, Antrim

Buffy Graffin

Buffy is our family dog,
She is brown in colour, with blue eyes,
She loves to eat, even pies and flies,
She's the best you've ever met,
You'd love her too if you saw her,
She barks but doesn't purr,
She's only four, but stays outside the door,
She has her own house,
Which we clean out all the time,
I'm glad Buffy is mine.

Beverley Graffin (8)
Millquarter Primary School, Antrim

Portstewart

I like going to Portstewart
In the summertime
I play in the Strand Park
Where I swing and climb

At the rockpools
I use my net
To try to catch a crab
But watch out, because they might grab

I see my friend, Owen
And we laugh and play
Let's go to Portstewart
And have a happy day!

Caolán McCloy (9)
Millquarter Primary School, Antrim

In The Swimming Pool

Splish, splash, splish, splash
In the swimming pool
Lots of water all nice and cool
Swimming up and down the place
Splashing water in people's face
Jumping in and climbing out
Children laugh, play and shout
Sliding down the twirling slide
What a good water ride
Children laughing in delight
Monday is our swimming pool night!

Oisín Duffin (8)
Millquarter Primary School, Antrim

My Dog

Some dogs are nice
Some dogs are bold
My dog is called Jessie
And she is as good as gold!

Michael Martin (7)
Millquarter Primary School, Antrim

My Dog

I have a dog that's red
He always wants to be fed
He hates the word bed
He likes to stay up instead
He likes to go on walks
And secretly can talk!

Luke Paul Devlin (8)
Millquarter Primary School, Antrim

Pastimes And Hobbies

There are lots of different pastimes and hobbies to do,
Which one do you like to do?
I like to play football and I like to swim,
I like art and I play camogie as well
When it's raining, I read a book or write a story.

Do you like to run or hop or jump or skip?
Or do you ride a bike, a scooter or a skateboard?
Or maybe you like to listen to music?
What do you like best?

There are lots of different pastimes and hobbies too,
Which one do you choose?

Ciara Madden (7)
Millquarter Primary School, Antrim

Sport

I like football, it is fun
Playing matches and scoring goals
With my friends.

I like boxing, it is cool!
Training on the punchbag,
Speedball and pads with my brother.

I like tennis, it keeps me fit
Running and hitting the ball over the net
To my sister on the other side.

I like sport
And sometimes I win!

Shane O'Neill (8)
Millquarter Primary School, Antrim

My Day At School

I say 'Hi,' to my friends each day at school.
A bus sits outside waiting to take us to the pool.
Everyone is happy as we get there on time.
Another day at Millquarter Primary school and everything is fine . . .

Eamon Kelly (7)
Millquarter Primary School, Antrim

My Baby Cousin

Rory is my cousin
He drinks bobos by the dozen
When he has a dirty nappy
He does not look very happy
He likes to laugh and giggle
And lie on the floor and wriggle
He laughs every time I read to him
From my nursery rhymes
That is the story of my cousin, Rory.

Aliesha McNally (8)
Millquarter Primary School, Antrim

Daddy

How I miss you, Daddy
When you go away
I miss your jokes, so funny they are
I can't let you go away.

You go to so many places
I can't name them all
You are so lucky, you've seen the world
I hope to be like you someday!

Patrick Magee (8)
Millquarter Primary School, Antrim

My Poem

I like lots of exercise
And good things that I can do
I also like to play football
And other things too!

Good food
I like lots of sweets
And lots and lots of chips
And I absolutely hate pips!

Órlaith Prenter (7)
Millquarter Primary School, Antrim

The River Foyle

It feels like a smooth river that has just been cleaned
It smells like a dirty, salty bag of crisps
The River Foyle looks like an enormous stormy black hole at night
The River Foyle is a light turquoise blue
The Foyle tastes like a rusty can of out-of-date baked beans
The Foyle sounds like your mummy saying,
'Shh, the baby's sleeping.'

Jack McClelland (9)
Newbuildings Primary School, Londonderry

The River Foyle

The River Foyle looks like light aqua blue
It feels like a melting ice cream
It sounds like a splashing wave coming towards the rocks
It tastes like goat's milk squirting in your eyes
It looks like a crystal mirror shining at you
It smells like bad breath coming out of your mouth.

Amy Killen (9)
Newbuildings Primary School, Londonderry

The River Foyle

The colour of the Foyle is turquoise blue with circles of silver
The River Foyle feels like a deep, cold swimming pool
The River Foyle sounds like a tiny stream flowing gently
                              down to the riverbank
The River Foyle smells like an old, dirty onion
The River Foyle tastes like a salty, disgusting drink
The River Foyle looks like a shiny mirror showing your reflection.

Alice McVeigh (8)
Newbuildings Primary School, Londonderry

The River Foyle

The River Foyle feels like a dripping tap
It sounds like my mum saying, *'Shh!'*
It tastes like an out-of-date carton of sour milk on a hot day
The River Foyle looks like a dirty, old mirror that has been polished
                              once every year
Its colour is a light blue turquoise
It smells like slurry that has just been spread over a muddy field!

Gillian Dunn (9)
Newbuildings Primary School, Londonderry

The River Foyle

The River Foyle smells like a rotten bowl of cabbage that has been
                              lying for days
It looks like a deep, old, mud bath that has never been cleaned
It sounds like a mouse squeaking that has just been stood on
                              by a person
The colour of the River Foyle is mostly blue, but it changes colours,
              like olive green, turquoise and mucky colours
I think it tastes like an out-of-date pack of cheese
It feels like a ball of melting snow!

Hannah Thompson (9)
Newbuildings Primary School, Londonderry

The River Foyle

It looks like a straight, clear mirror that's been polished every day
of the week
The colour of the River Foyle is a fabulous dark, royal, rich blue
The River Foyle tastes like an old, disgusting, left-over bottle
of flat soda water that someone has spat on
It sounds like a mad, raging whirlpool that's sucking up
the river furiously
The river feels like smooth sand rushing quietly down the
side of my hand
The Foyle smells like a messy, old, rotten garden with no
beautiful flowers or plants.

Mark Robinson (9)
Newbuildings Primary School, Londonderry

The River Foyle

It smells like a rusty old park
The Foyle looks like a damp old pair of nappies
The River Foyle could be a gloomy, mucky brown
It tastes like a pot of sour milk and goat's cheese
The Foyle sounds like thunder hitting deeply into the rocks
The Foyle feels like a leaking tap in my bathroom.

Lewis Lecky (8)
Newbuildings Primary School, Londonderry

The River Foyle

The river tastes very fishy like rotting salmon
The river is a very light turquoise
It feels like a very dirty river
It sounds like someone whispering to another person
It smells like someone did windies in the river
It looks like a deep puddle.

Ross Thompson (9)
Newbuildings Primary School, Londonderry

The River Foyle

It feels like a cold blue defrosted leaking tap
It sounds like a huge wave crashing at the rocks
The River Foyle smells like the bin lorry coming past
The River Foyle tastes like boiled-up cabbage with goat's cheese
The Foyle is sometimes turquoise blue and sometimes brown
The River Foyle looks like a dirty, old, muddy bath.

Justin McFaul (9)
Newbuildings Primary School, Londonderry

The River Foyle

The River Foyle looks like a dirty, old-fashioned swimming pool
The colour of the River Foyle is dirty and black
The River Foyle feels like a blueberry pie all squashed up
The River Foyle sounds like waves rushing into the bank of the river
The River Foyle tastes like a dirty, muddy swamp.

Alex Warke (9)
Newbuildings Primary School, Londonderry

The River Foyle

A gloomy, dark brown colour
It feels like a leaking, old tap dripping
It smells like a pair of old, dirty socks
It looks like a shiny, blue, clear river
It sounds like a squeaking mouse getting stood on by a boy or girl
It tastes like rusty oil that came off the trucks
And it hasn't been cleaned up.

Ross Dougherty (8)
Newbuildings Primary School, Londonderry

The River Foyle

It looks like a dirty, smelly swamp
It smells like a zoo that hasn't been cleaned out in four months
The River Foyle tastes like hairspray just been sprayed
                                                           into your mouth
It sounds like the thunder dashing against the rocks
The River Foyle is olive green and mucky
The River Foyle feels like ice cream melting on your hands.

Reece Sproule (9)
Newbuildings Primary School, Londonderry

The River Foyle

It smells like someone hasn't brushed their teeth for a week
The River Foyle's colour is like a mucky, old brown on a rusty bicycle
It sounds like my teacher's pen squeaking on the whiteboard
The River Foyle looks like a long strip of tinfoil that has been
                                                     crumpled up and flattened again
It tastes like goat's cheese melted in the sun on a summer's day
It feels like the sand dripping down an egg timer!

Hollie Wallace (9)
Newbuildings Primary School, Londonderry

The River Foyle

The River Foyle sounds like huge splashing waves clashing
                                                      against the rocks
It tastes like a rotten, old bag of crisps
It looks like a silvery crystal mirror
The River Foyle is a beautiful silvery-bluish colour
The River Foyle feels like an old, cold, leaking tap
The River Foyle smells like a smelly old zoo that has not been
                                                      cleaned out for three years!

Nicole Rochester (9)
Newbuildings Primary School, Londonderry

The River Foyle

It looks like a crystal mirror reflection from the beautiful shining sun
It smells like an old, dirty zoo that hasn't been cleaned for months
The River Foyle tastes like soda water and a rusty, old robot on
                                                            a windy day
The colours of the River Foyle are light and dark blue, turquoise,
                                  silvery, aqua and crystal clear like the sun
It feels like a leaking, dripping cold tap which would not stop
                                          on a cold and stormy day
The River Foyle sounds like thunder, splashing waves rushing
                                          and crashing on the rocks
It is like a hurricane on a really stormy day and night.

Brittany Craig (9)
Newbuildings Primary School, Londonderry

The River Foyle

The River Foyle looks like a crusty, burnt bit of toast in wintertime
The River Foyle sounds like a mad dinosaur trying to get out of a
                                          cage on a stormy morning
The river is the colour of mud-brown when it starts to rain
The nasty, old river tastes like an out-of-date cup of iced tea
                                    that has been sitting open for months
The Foyle feels like a non-stop leaking tap on your hands
And it smells like a football top covered in sweat and sewage.

James Philip McClelland (9)
Newbuildings Primary School, Londonderry

The River Foyle

The river is light blue, but it is white in bits of it
It tastes like a bit of old goat's cheese that has been spat on
The Foyle sounds like a hundred bombs going off at the same time
The river feels like the leftovers from my dinner with cabbage in it
The river smells like a baby's old, stinky nappy
It looks like a mirror that is reflecting right back at you.

James Nutt (8)
Newbuildings Primary School, Londonderry

The River Foyle

It tastes like sour milk on a hot day
The river sounds like splashing waves
It feels like a leaking, rusty old tap
The river smells like a week-old nappy that hasn't been changed
The river looks like a mirror that would not break
It is like a mucky brown that is so *black*.

Charlie Johnston (9)
Newbuildings Primary School, Londonderry

The Famine

It's a terrible day for the Irish
As the famine has raised its ugly head.
It appears to be invincible!
I feel I don't have much time
As I'm fighting a losing battle.

I'm getting weaker by the day
And as I utter my last words
And take my last breath in this world,
I am engulfed by death
And at last, I'm free!

Niall Keenan (10)
New Row Primary School, Castledawson

Black

Black is the colour of night
Black is the colour of an alleyway
Black is the colour of death
Black is the colour of sadness
Black is the colour of a deep hole
Black is the colour of disappointment.

Oisin Lennon (10)
New Row Primary School, Castledawson

What Is Snow?

Snow is the ground
Painted ceramic white.

Show is a feather falling
From God's cushion.

Snow is a sheep
Getting sheared by a farmer.

Snow is a blanket
Covering me and you.

Snow is a cloud
Breaking into tiny pieces.

Snow is a glass of milk
Descending down your body.

Rian Connery (10)
New Row Primary School, Castledawson

The Fateful Famine

These aren't the good times
Where the potatoes thrive
They're all blushed with grey
And it's hard to survive.

My mother is dying
There's nothing we can do
She's just moaning on the haystacks
And crippled with the flu.

My family have perished
Due to this fateful year
I'm stuck at home
Wiping away a tear.

I take a look around
For what seems the last time
I've just become a victim
Of this terrible crime.

Gareth Armstrong (11)
New Row Primary School, Castledawson

The Famine

I take a look around the town
And smell the sickness in the air.
I have nothing left to eat
So I have to starve.

There is no way I can survive
All we have is poisoned potatoes.
I'm going to die soon
At least then I can rest in peace.

My mother's dying from the fever
And my father's away to the roadworks.
My family is getting weaker
With each passing day.

All we can do now is wait
For Father to return.
The pain is becoming unbearable
And I'm beginning to lose the will to live.

The sickness is sweeping through our town
And leaving corpses in its wake.
I pray to God that I will not join
This ever-growing death list.

Pearse Loughran (10)
New Row Primary School, Castledawson

Darkness Engulfs Me!

The famine has arrived with such ferocity,
People are dying from hunger and disease,
I'd be better off leaving this desperate land.

I know I soon will be joining my sister,
On a journey with no return,
For famine is slowly suffocating me
And I find I can't breathe,
Then darkness engulfs me!

Cara O'Hagan (11)
New Row Primary School, Castledawson

Goodbye, Farewell

The famine is here
It's coming to get us
We've all got the fever
We're dying quick!

The potatoes are rotting
And we've nothing to eat!
And oh no!
We will have to go to the workhouse!

And now my journey has ended
I am heading into darkness
I take my last glance
Goodbye, farewell.

Caoimhe McGoldrick (11)
New Row Primary School, Castledawson

Famine Killer

I've reached my destination
And I'm ready to strike.
I roam this Emerald Isle
Searching for my prey.
The poor are easy targets
They have no escape.
So I take them, one by one
Until I am satisfied
That I have brought this country
To its knees.

Daniel O'Neill (11)
New Row Primary School, Castledawson

Horrid Life

The famine has descended upon us
And we are starving.
Dad has gone to the roadworks
Mum is broken-hearted
With the loss of her child.
I'm getting weaker by the day
And I'm losing the will to live.
My time here on Earth is coming to an end
And I look forward to seeing my sister again once more.
The lights are fading
So I must say farewell.

Daneka O'Hagan (11)
New Row Primary School, Castledawson

Down Death Lane

Down Death Lane
That's the way I am going
And so many people
Are going my way.
No food, no water
No happy memories to share.
And at the end
Of this journey,
There'll be . . .
No pain, no suffering,
No nothing
Anymore!

Emma McKeever (10)
New Row Primary School, Castledawson

The Famine

Life is hard in this cruel world
Quick, the landlord is coming!
Watch out!
He is knocking at the door!

I'm stuck here while the lucky ones
Set sail to America.
I'm undecided in what I should do.
I'm alone in my cottage,
Sick and exasperated,
In this godforsaken country.

Finally, I see the light . . .
I know that I'm going to a better place
To see my family once more.

Brigid McMullan (11)
New Row Primary School, Castledawson

My Time Is Up

My time on the Earth is coming to an end
For the wind of death is blowing in my direction.
I say goodbye to my family
As I begin my upward journey.
I wish you happiness
And I hope you don't end up like me.
Please remember me
And know that I will always love you.
Goodbye for now.

Maria Doherty (10)
New Row Primary School, Castledawson

The Famine

Death is coming,
Breathing upon me,
Screaming out my name.

The light appears
And it's shining in my direction,
I pull my body up with all my strength.

I'm walking towards the light,
All pain has eased,
I'm floating ever so lightly.

I see my family and friends,
I hope this wonderful place
Has no end.

Niamh Bell (11)
New Row Primary School, Castledawson

Bling, Bling

I'm a cool white rapper
Just doing my thing.
I've got shiny gold watches
And some serious bling!

I've got lots of money
And baggy waggy pants.
Let's go to a party
And dance, dance, dance!

I'm going home now
I've had lots of fun.
This is the end
My rap is done!

Siobhan Burke (10)
New Row Primary School, Castledawson

Christmas Day

On Christmas Day, we all . . .
Wake up in a good mood because of the snow
We get dressed
Go out in the snow
Make snow angels
Have good fun
The snow goes away
Let it snow! Oh, let it snow!
The snow falls down
Hooray! Hooray!
Look out my window
Snow blizzard today
Go away! Go away!

Caitlin Huston (8)
Our Lady's Girls' Primary School, Belfast

Snow

Snow is beautiful and nice to behold
But on the pinkies, rather cold
In the heat it will disappear
Only to come another year.

Lauren Hamilton (8)
Our Lady's Girls' Primary School, Belfast

Snow

I love snow so soft and white
It falls to the ground without a sound
Sometimes it falls through the night
Oh, what a beautiful sight!
Children play all around
Building snowmen on the ground
When the sun comes out it melts away
Then there is no more play.

Emily Murphy (9)
Our Lady's Girls' Primary School, Belfast

Snow, Snow, Snow

Snow, snow, all around
Just like a blanket on the ground
As I look out of my window and see
All the children playing cheerfully
Having brilliant snowball fights with my friends
I love it when winter comes around
I hate to say goodbye to the winter
Because there's no snow on the ground.

Chantelle Markey (8)
Our Lady's Girls' Primary School, Belfast

Snowflake

Snowflake, oh snowflake,
You are nice and soft
Falling from the sky
And on the ground you lie.
Your colour is white
When it is nice and bright
Then you sadly melt away
And come back the next day.
The next day when it snows
It's going to be very cold.
The snow is on my car,
Look! Look! Look!
It's way down deep.
Yesterday there was some
The snow falls down and away
Every day.

Kaitlin Rock (9)
Our Lady's Girls' Primary School, Belfast

Snow

I love snow
Snow is bright
It lights up the night

We all have snowball fights
We all build snowmen
Big ones and small ones
Some have carrot noses
Some have hats and scarves

I like to slide in it
Sometimes I fall on my bum
And everyone has a good laugh

I like the feel of snow
Out the window you see it fall
It really looks like cotton balls.

Rachael Anderson (8)
Our Lady's Girls' Primary School, Belfast

Snow

When I look at snow
I see all white
Then I look more closely
I see little snowflakes
They look like little stars
Stars falling from the night sky
When I feel snow
I feel soft snow
The snow is cold
If I hold it too long
My hands get sore and bright red.

Monica Delaney (9)
Our Lady's Girls' Primary School, Belfast

Snow Is Falling

Dancing, running, having fun
Jumping up and splashing down
What's that on the ground?
They're snowflakes, let's stick out our tongues
Jumping, laughing in the snow
Oh, it's chilly!
Get on your hat, scarf and gloves
Then you can build a snowman with a big nose
It's very cold and getting dark
Let's go inside!

Danielle Stewart (9)
Our Lady's Girls' Primary School, Belfast

Fog

I do not like the fog
It really scares me
Because it is smoky and cold
And I am not too sure
Just which way to go!

When I am walking
And I hear footsteps
I look to see who is there
But all I can see are shadows
And that is when I am really scared.

I really start to worry
And I try so hard to hurry
But as the shadows near
They become clear
It's not a monster or alien
It's my neighbour with his dog, Sabien.

Nicole Corbett (9)
Our Lady's Girls' Primary School, Belfast

Fog

The fog falls all around me,
Covering everything nearby
My world has disappeared now,
I feel a little frightened with no one else around.

But wait, as my mind wanders
No one can see me
I could be a twenty-two foot giant
Or even a rock star
Or really anything I want to be!

I am invisible,
But soon the fog will clear, I know,
So I will just enjoy my imaginary life,
For another little while or so.

Kirstyn Smith (9)
Our Lady's Girls' Primary School, Belfast

Snow

The beautiful white snow
And the lovely shimmering snowflakes
Always fall in the wintertime,

As the snow falls
The children laugh and play,

As the snow falls
The children have a good day,

In the wintertime
Wrap up warm and have a great day!

Fiona McGoran (9)
Our Lady's Girls' Primary School, Belfast

Fog

It is foggy and very cold
It can be dangerous, so I'm told.
Putting on a scarf and a hat
I may be careful I don't stand on the cat.
It is misty, I can barely see
I can't really see in front of me.
I feel alone in the street
Now I feel my heart begin to beat.
Hearing strange noises all around
If I get lost, will I be found?
Suddenly, the fog begins to lift
The grey mist starts to drift.
Now I can see in front of me
I am so happy that I can see!

Morgan Kelly (9)
Our Lady's Girls' Primary School, Belfast

Fog

The fog is cold,
The fog is thick,
The fog is dark
And the fog surrounds me.

The fog makes people look like shadows
Car lights are dim
The fog is black
The fog is annoying
The fog is grey
I think the fog
Is a giant smoking a cigar!

Rebecca McLaverty (9)
Our Lady's Girls' Primary School, Belfast

Fog

Come outside until you see,
Just how scary it can be.
The fog has come,
It's cold and dark,
You can't see the people in the park.
The sky is grey, misty too,
It's really creepy
For me and you.

Emer Ward (8)
Our Lady's Girls' Primary School, Belfast

Christmas

It's this time of year
It is crystal clear
And everyone is having fun
But not in the sun!

The whole place is white
And I'm snuggled up tight
The place is covered in snow
I know!

It's Christmas time
People drinking wine
We're eating turkey
Now we're perky.

It's time for bed
I'm a sleepyhead
I fall asleep
There's not a peep
Everyone's quiet 'cause I'm asleep
Shh!

Sorcha McCarthy (10)
Our Lady's Girls' Primary School, Belfast

New Year's Eve

N ew Year's Eve is when you have fun
E veryone hugs each other
W hen people dance with a partner

Y ou will know it is New Year's Eve because people will be drunk
    Because they're on their knees
E veryone will be eating turkey
A ll the adults break the crackers
R unning around the children go
S nowball fights all around

E veryone is getting sleepy
V iolent dogs are barking
E veryone is now in bed.

Seana Doran (11)
Our Lady's Girls' Primary School, Belfast

Little Star

Little star shining so bright,
Guiding people like a light,
So far in the sky,
Cannot touch it, it's so high.

It twinkles,
It shimmers,
It moves so slow,
It has a vibrant glow.

If you listen,
You can almost hear it glisten,
You can see the spark,
In the deep, black dark.

Amy McAnespie (11)
Our Lady's Girls' Primary School, Belfast

Fairies

There are lots and lots of different types
They like to go and take some flights
Up in the sky, day and night
But only sometimes in the light

But this creature won't hurt you
Here's what, I'll give you a clue
They've got wings so wide
And sometimes they like to hide

So you always must be sure
That you don't step where they lie
And you'd be lucky
If they said, *'Hi!'*

So, if you don't know what I am talking about
The next is a must
There are three things you will need
Faith, trust and pixie dust.

Fairies.

Clare McGibbon (10)
Our Lady's Girls' Primary School, Belfast

My Dog, Tara

My dog, Tara, is oh, so nice,
She has sugar and a little spice.
Whenever I see her, it brightens my day,
The clouds in the sky all roll away.

She would never hurt anyone,
She would never bite,
She truly is my one delight.

She is so playful
And I love her so,
She completes our family
And she comes with us wherever we go.

Niamh Scott (11)
Our Lady's Girls' Primary School, Belfast

School Is Cool

School is cool
School is fun
School is for everyone!

You like fun, you like play
So get up and work your day
Do your maths, English and science
Just think of it like flying.

Before you know it
You're halfway through it
Just have a break
Eat your cake
Have fun and play.

Go back to your class
And have a blast
Do your history, geography or religion
Just think like a party.

Then have your lunch
With a munch, munch
Do some work, then go home
Have fun and play and that's your day!

Colleen Doherty (11)
Our Lady's Girls' Primary School, Belfast

My Poem

C is for caterpillar, delicate and colourful
O is for owl, fluffy and elegant
R is for rabbit, loveable and cuddly
R is for rat, small and ugly
I is for insect, creepy and small
N is for Nelly, the big elephant, big and smelly
A is for antelope, big and bright.

Corrina Brady (11)
Our Lady's Girls' Primary School, Belfast

Winter's All Around

If you look twice
And see some ice
Snowflakes on the ground
Then you know winter's all around.

Stars twinkle in the sky
As Santa's reindeer passes on by
The snow is like a white sheet
Christmas pudding tastes so sweet.

Christmas Eve is here at last
Enjoy the party, have a blast
The tree is so high
It looks like it touches the sky.

It's finally here
Time to go to bed
I'm so glad I'm warm and tucked in tight
On the cold winter's night.

Melissa Keenan (10)
Our Lady's Girls' Primary School, Belfast

Football Crazy

The thrill of the match
The keeper will catch
Any strikes coming his way
Ronaldo runs past
Extremely fast
Scoring the goal of the day!

The fans all cheer
Drinking some beer
And have a laugh
But don't act daft
Fans are mates
They all need dates
And they are walking out the gates.

Una Kelly (10)
Our Lady's Girls' Primary School, Belfast

The World Of War

1939 was the year,
The end of the world came near,
Hitler was the man who was to rule,
When the whole world came to duel.

With the Nazis at his back
He was far on his track
Hitler was full of hate
He imprisoned Jews at a terrible rate.

Soon he was to destroy,
All the different lands with joy,
After that he was soon gone,
People were glad, no more *bomb!*

Hannah Cartmill (11)
Our Lady's Girls' Primary School, Belfast

Winnie The Pooh

A humble bear, plump and yellow
Who is smarter than you would think
Is friends with a small, little fellow
Who's shy and bright pink!

They live in the Hundred Acre Wood
Where they have lots of adventures and fun
With honey as their favourite food
They have picnics in the brilliant sun.

The day starts to end
And the two friends are asleep fast
Another day just around the bend
What a day it was that just passed!

Ciara Bradley (11)
Our Lady's Girls' Primary School, Belfast

Jack Frost

He comes skiing at night,
In fearsome fright,
His garments are blue and cool,
He comes to you with a pot of stew,
He sits and waits with his plates,
When you awake to see his skates,
You see his stew turned to goo,
You go and get ready for school,
He freezes with his fingers,
As the cold winter lingers,
As the crisp, cold day ends,
I stay inside with friends.

Breanne McAuley (11)
Our Lady's Girls' Primary School, Belfast

Walking Home On A Snowy Evening

I was walking home, very warm,
Then I saw a snowstorm,
I got caught out in it,
I even got a frost bit,
I got home safely,
Then my mummy was glad to see me,
I asked her to make me a cup of tea,
Then I sat on the settee,
I called my dog,
But I could not see her in the fog,
I called my mummy for a torchlight,
But it was too bright,
I called her, she came over to me,
I said to her, 'You are my number one doggie!'

Francesca Winters (10)
Our Lady's Girls' Primary School, Belfast

The Christmas Holiday Cheer

C hristmas is a special time of year
H olly berries are decorating Christmas cheer
R eindeer pull the sleigh and then they're on their way
I cicles dance on the wind and they say, 'Hey!'
S anta Claus is coming to deliver toys to good girls and boys
T ry to be good, but make a little bit of noise
M others go out to buy
A ngels do not like to do this and then they sigh
S leigh bells ring and land on your roof.

Rachel Cartmill (11)
Our Lady's Girls' Primary School, Belfast

My Dog, Henry

Small, chubby, golden feet,
Eyes like buttons you want to eat!
Velvet ears, all black and brown,
Wet nose with a funny frown.

He loves to play in the garden,
Getting dirty and chasing leaves,
All excited and delighted,
To get out in the breeze.

Next up, is the bath tub,
He really enjoys that too!
Getting wet and next blow-dried,
He then smells like shampoo!

He waddles down the stairs, in his playful way,
After his adventurous, tiresome day!
He jumps up upon my knee to have a snooze,
Dreaming about a lovely, tasty pair of shoes!

Tory Henry (11)
Our Lady's Girls' Primary School, Belfast

The Stray

Abandoned, neglected, all alone,
Wandering the streets to find its way home.
Its owner has left it with nowhere to go,
Left by itself in the rain and the snow.
It is searching the dumps for leftover food,
Food that is rotten and that tastes no good.
The dog has a limp, its ear is sore too,
Its teeth badly ache and it's got terrible flu.
A bright little child spots the poor, lonely dog,
She can just see it as it walks through the fog.
She shouts to her mother, 'Mammy, look there!'
The mother looks sadly at its long, filthy hair.
As the child goes to touch it, she pulls her away,
From the lonely, hungry, abandoned stray.
It is left all alone in the wind and the sleet,
That poor little puppy that wanders my street.

Hannah Ferrin (11)
Our Lady's Girls' Primary School, Belfast

Birthday

B irthday parties are the best
I f they are greater than the rest
R estless games are so much fun
T o play outside in the bright sun
H appy birthday because you're number one
D id you get lots of things
A necklace perhaps or maybe some rings?
Y ou just need one more, someone to shout
Happy Birthday!

Nicole Service (11)
Our Lady's Girls' Primary School, Belfast

Me!

E very day I try to respect my friends and family
I treat others the way I like to be treated
R emember to always be well mannered, polite, caring, respectful and pleasant
I f people remembered to use these manners, what a wonderful world it would be
N obody is perfect, but still remember to always use your manners
N ever disrespect your elders or your friends or your family.

Eirinn Murphy (10)
Our Lady's Girls' Primary School, Belfast

Alley Cat

Late in the alley lurks an old tabby cat,
He sits and he purrs with his old top hat.
No bed to lie, but contented still,
He lets out a cry, an awful shrill.

The clock strikes twelve,
The moon brightly glistens,
Suddenly it's quiet, the cat stops and listens.
Nothing to hear but the voices in the distance,
Next thing I knew, cats were there in an instant!

They gathered around in a circle it seemed,
In the night sky above, the moon brightly beamed.
When down upon them, as if in a dream,
They feasted on fish and on mice and on cream.

After the feast, when all the cats left,
The old alley cat lay down for a rest.
With his tummy full, he was feeling fat,
He perched his head on his old top hat.

Lauren Benson (10)
Our Lady's Girls' Primary School, Belfast

A Windy Night

The wind blows through the sky
And the leaves start to fly
As the clouds go passing by
The wind starts to whirl
And the trees start to twirl
Then the leaves start to swirl.

Cara McDonnell (7)
Our Lady's Girls' Primary School, Belfast

Poems

Our homework tonight is to write a poem
About anything we want
But nothing seem to spring to mind
My brain screams, 'I can't!'

I get my pen and paper out
And put my thinking cap on,
I know I can do it if I try,
I just need to switch myself on!

Enya Lawlor (10)
Our Lady's Girls' Primary School, Belfast

A Windy Night

Windows rattling
Washing, whipping on the washing line
Branches breaking
Leaves rustling
A windy night in wintertime.

Meaghan Smyth (7)
Our Lady's Girls' Primary School, Belfast

My Name

K is for kind, the person that I am and always will be
A is for all, that's what I put into everything I do
T is for together, that's the way I like everybody to stay
I is for important, that's what you and me are
E is for everything, that's always important to me

B is for bright beautiful mornings I wake up to every day
U is for the universe, so lovely that we live in
R is for the robin hopping about on Christmas morning
N is for nuts that little squirrels love to eat
S is for the sunshine that brightens up our day.

Katie Burns (11)
Our Lady's Girls' Primary School, Belfast

The New Arrival

One day, my mummy said to me,
'You're going to be a big sister, now how do you feel?'
I then said, in an excited voice,
'Is it a boy or a girl? Do I have a choice?'
Mum then said, 'It might be a boy, all dressed in blue,
Or a beautiful little princess, just like you.'
I've been an only child for almost ten years
And the thought of a baby does fill me with fear.
Will it keep me awake with its cries in the night?
Or will it break all my toys? That fills me with fright.
My mummy's tummy is getting bigger and I'm feeling happy,
But please Mummy, don't make me change its nappy.

Megan Dobbin (9)
Our Lady's Girls' Primary School, Belfast

Nature

When I look at the sun, I see he has a grin
When I look at the moon, I see she looks so sad
When I look at the waves, I see they look angry
When I look at the sand, I see they are bossed
When I look at the grass, I see it likes to sway
When I look at the mud, I see it is so gooey
When I look at a tree, I see his muscular shape
When I look at the stars, I see how they twinkle
When I look at the sky, I see it is dark and grey
When I look at nature, I see how creation looks.

Maureen Davidson (11)
Our Lady's Girls' Primary School, Belfast

Winter

Looking out my window in the darkness of the night
I saw beautiful white lights falling softly to the ground
I ran to the door and outside I went to play in the snow
Oh, how beautiful and soft was the snow and I began to glow
At the thought of all the fun I would have
Throwing snowballs one by one
Trying to hit all my friends as they ran and ran
Having lots of fun in the winter wonderland that had begun
All this snow that had fallen way up high from the sky
Had made beautiful lights in the darkness of night.

Grace McCorry (10)
Our Lady's Girls' Primary School, Belfast

My Fluffy Pal

My fluffy pal is such a treat,
She likes to hide under the sheet.
My fluffy pal is so cute,
When the hoover goes on, she's out like a shoot.
My fluffy pal's name is Pepper,
But people call her Depper.
Sometimes she can be a brat,
Oh, did I mention?
She's a cat!

Sarah Marley (10)
Our Lady's Girls' Primary School, Belfast

Clodagh

C lodagh is my name
L ike a famous singer
O range is my favourite colour
D oesn't mean I don't like any other
A pples are my favourite fruit
G reen and red are the colours of apples
H ealthy for us is our fruit.

Clodagh McIlkenny (10)
Our Lady's Girls' Primary School, Belfast

My Furry Friend

My furry friend, he is just a dog
We walk around and splash in bogs
We put on his lead and go for a run
When we go out, we have such fun!
He is two years old, so small and cute
Before his first bark, he was dead-on mute
His name is Jack, he loves to play
He begs to play, every day!

Courtney McIlkenny (9)
Our Lady's Girls' Primary School, Belfast

I . . .

I love to jump,
I love to dance,
I love to put ice in my sister's pants!

I hate to run,
I hate to think,
I even hate the colour pink!

I think you rock,
I think you rule,
But I think I put the 'cool' in school!

I wish I was pretty,
I wish I was rich,
Wouldn't that be a wonderful wish?

Wishes are wonderful,
Wishes are fine,
What is a wish if it cannot be mine?

Grace McLaughlin (9)
Our Lady's Girls' Primary School, Belfast

Windy Nights

Trees are rustling
Wind is whistling
Through my cold ears
Round and round the merry-go-round
Leaves are dancing on the ground
In and round the merry-go-round
People are fussing
To do their shopping
I love the wind and the wind loves me.

Julie Donnelly (6)
Our Lady's Girls' Primary School, Belfast

Windy Night

The clouds were dark
And the sky was grey and dull.
The leaves were falling off the trees
And the wind was blowing them away.
It was damp and wet,
Tomorrow night will be the same, I bet.

Sophie Teer (7)
Our Lady's Girls' Primary School, Belfast

Windy Night

It was a windy night
It gave me a fright
The wind was howling
Like a dog growling
The trees were shaking
A lot of noise the wind was making
I was tucked up in bed
And there I stayed, snug as a bug on a rug.

Emily McGearty (6)
Our Lady's Girls' Primary School, Belfast

The Little Princess

There once was a little princess,
She always played fancy dress,
She always had loads of sweets
And had friends who brought lots of treats.
They played night and day
And the princess would say,
'I hope you can all stay
And play till the next day!'

Aimee McLarnon (7)
Our Lady's Girls' Primary School, Belfast

Windy Night

I see the wind rushing through trees
I see the wind brushing the leaves
I feel the wind lifting me off my feet
Then I hear the wind rapping on my door.

Amy-Jane Clarke (7)
Our Lady's Girls' Primary School, Belfast

My Smelly Fish

I've found a fish deep down my toilet
Think it must have come from the sewers
Because it's smelly and shabby
You can smell it a mile away.

I fed it on many things, like
Chips, cod liver oil and bookworms
He kept swimming away and saying
'I don't need that, I need something else.'

It made a home
With toilet roll and water
It is quite sad
I feel sorry for it.

If you believed, would you please
Come to my house to see this fish
It would like you to come
And see it one day!

Nicole Amy Martin (10)
Rosetta Primary School, Belfast

The Fire

Hear the sound of a match being struck
Against its safe home
Then lighting a defenceless piece of coal
And grabbing its true form away
Up goes the blaze trapped in its steel jail
Coughing and spluttering, trying to stay alive
And then better and its calm
Munching and chewing at the extra parts
Thrown at it, getting bigger and bigger
The crackling sound of unneeded paper
Being wasted for a fire
Then, as it's going to sleep,
The carpet awakens and all is dead.

Nathan Quinn (11)
Rosetta Primary School, Belfast

The Seasons

Autumn has awakened,
The trees start to panic,
They chatter amongst each other,
'Today's the day I might lose my leaves,'
One of the leaves interrupts,
'We get to dance around the garden soon,'
After playing hide-and-seek with their friends,
The leaves lie down like a blanket, keeping in the warmth.

Rebecca Laverty (11)
Rosetta Primary School, Belfast

The Wildlife Parade

The sun yawned one morning and peered down to the glade.
The flowers moaned as there was really not much shade.
Bluebells giggled while picnicking by the river,
The whistling wind makes trees and long blades of grass quiver.

Daffodils boasted about their leaves and their vibrancy,
Leaves and twigs go around in a lovely circle dance.
All the wildlife gathers round to see this little parade
A fancy waiter frog gives out shots of acornade.

The moon appears
And everyone cheers
And crickets start to leap
While the moon sings them a sweet lullaby
Gently off to sleep.

Caitlin McNally (10)
Rosetta Primary School, Belfast

In The Garden

I have a garden outside
The flowers open with a yawn
The wind howls
And the door of the shed
Jumps off its hinges with a bang
The leaves start to dance
They are performing
Like it is a competition
Grass pokes holes in the tarmac
Trying to see the outside world
The bushes shiver in the cold
The fence sways in the wind
The water fountain cries
And I sit inside
What a wonderful sight!

Kyle Hurst (10)
Rosetta Primary School, Belfast

Lonely Tree

The tree woke up with panic
Wondering how it lost all of its leaves
He knocks on all the windows nearby
Wondering where all his leaves have gone
He remembers himself running around the park
He spots all of his leaves under another tree
He thinks he must have snatched them
And then he looks for weeks at his bare branches
And feels all alone
Before long, he finds a bunch of new leaves blooming
He was as happy as a child at their 16th birthday
He has finally got his leaves back.

John Lindsay (11)
Rosetta Primary School, Belfast

The Angry Storm!

As the thunder grumbles
And makes our Earth rumble,
The lightning dazzles and dances,
But you can only get,
A few glances.
The wind whistles
And the rain weeps,
Oh, up darkness creeps.
It seems brightness has been snatched away!

Hazel Peacock (10)
Rosetta Primary School, Belfast

Winter Is Here!

As the snowflakes dance around the garden,
The wind sings a gentle lullaby.
Winter is on its way to welcome the new day,
The leaves have fallen and have vanished away.
As the garden begins to sleep
And feels itself shiver,
The grass lies down getting ready for winter.

Courtney Hewitt (11)
Rosetta Primary School, Belfast

The Leaves!

The leaves jump up
In the sky.

The leaves run
Like the wind.

The leaves run
Around the tree.

The trees walk
In the wind.

The wind
Blows the trees.

The trees dance.

The leaves and the trees
Dream.

Yuki Mok (10)
Rosetta Primary School, Belfast

The Storm

The rain hammered down on the ground outside
The thunder howled over the storm
Suddenly, the lightning, with a *boom*, struck a tree
It hurtled down and smashed onto the ground
Another *boom* and another tree falls
This time, it crashes with a high-pitched crack.

Peter Foreman (11)
Rosetta Primary School, Belfast

The Storm

The air moaned as the wind whistled
The clouds coughed out rain
The oak tree knocked on my window
The rain thumped on my roof
The thunder and lightning roared
The sea smashed and bashed against the rocks.

Adam Gribben (11)
Rosetta Primary School, Belfast

My House

The TV screamed at the clock
The remote cried a lot
The trumpet talked to the lamp
Who thought he was the champ
As a person walked in
The chair chewed up the pillow
And the door cried when it was slammed.

Ryan Biggerstaff (11)
Rosetta Primary School, Belfast

Monster Garden

The wind began to rage in my garden
It was windy all day
As the leaves went out to play
They whispered around the garden
As the leaf monster ran over the hill
The leaves crunched on the ground
A storm had come
The branches shouted in the storm
Then the storm had stopped
The monster was not real
It was the leaves in the wind.

Megan Cotter (10)
Rosetta Primary School, Belfast

I Am Water

I run very fast
I cannot stop
I fall off a cliff
I land in bed
I got sucked up
I fall into a mouth
I keep running
At the speed of light
I took a different path
I came out of a hole
I was in a glass
And that was the end of me.

Jordan McWilliams (11)
Rosetta Primary School, Belfast

Caolán

Caolán is my little brother,
My only one, there is no other.
He likes to play and laugh and run,
Together we have lots of fun.

He's really cute and cuddly too
And loves to hear our cows go *moo!*
He wears his boots to splash in the puddles
And loves to get big, warm cuddles.

Caolán is very special to me,
We have lots of fun in our house by the sea.
He's my perfect little baby brother,
He is my world - thank you, Mother.

Patrick Quinn (11)
St Ciaran's Primary School, Cushendun

Ben

Ben is playful, happy and mad,
The only dog we've ever had.
He is good at chasing sheep,
But sometimes he just lands in a heap!

He likes to run beside the tractor,
But we know he'll come back after.
At times he comes home very late,
Because he likes to play with his mates.

He lives in a shed with Mitch and Jip,
Unfortunately at times, he gives a nip.
We got him down in County Tyrone,
I am so glad that he is now our own!

Rachael McNeill (11)
St Ciaran's Primary School, Cushendun

Anything

We have to write a poem about anything,
So, I'm thinking and hoping that my brain will go *ping!*
And suddenly, it will all become clear,
I'm going to write about . . . oh, dear, oh, dear!

I'm sucking my pen and biting my nails,
'Can't I write something?' my poor hand wails.
Now I'm biting my pen and sucking my nails,
Still, the old brain feels, once again it fails.

'Oh, hurry up!' my hand says with a hiss,
Think of all the fun we might just miss!
'I'm trying! I'm trying! Honest, I am!'
Announces my brain, 'Would you please remain calm?'

Oh, I'll just give it up, I'm no poet, you know,
I just can't seem to . . . go with the flow.
Perhaps it would be easier to climb Mount Everest?
Or in all the universe, make a robot the cleverest!

Anna McKay (11)
St Ciaran's Primary School, Cushendun

My Cat, Fluffy

My cat, Fluffy, is so black, yet so white,
Always so cute, but sometimes not bright.
I love him a lot and he loves me too,
He looks so scared when the cows go, 'Moo!'

Fluffy is so warm and lots of fun too,
He is only little, not fit for a zoo.
He's so lazy, he would sleep anywhere,
He is lovely and soft, just like my teddy bear!

Eileen Magee (11)
St Ciaran's Primary School, Cushendun

Thumper

I have a pet rabbit who's called Thumper,
He likes to bite and pull on my jumper.
He likes to eat his favourite food,
Because it puts him in a better mood.

He runs around the garden mad,
This makes me very cross and a little sad.
Thumper is my favourite pet,
I can safely say, he is the best rabbit yet!

Lauren McHugh (11)
St Ciaran's Primary School, Cushendun

My Winter Poem!

I just love winter
Because I can throw some snowballs without a splinter
When we do a snowball fight
Some people get a fright

In winter, I love to play
And I'm normally outside all day
I love hot cocoa
Then do the moco

The snowman sat
Big and fat
Fun I am
I stay very calm

We love to snowball fight
All night!

Megan McKenna (10)
St Mary's Primary School, Draperstown

What I Think Of Winter

Winter is lots of fun
Lots and lots for everyone
Winter is kind of blowy
Sometimes even a bit snowy

Winter is very white
Also the time for a snowball fight
My hands are cold, so I give them a blow
It's all because of the snow

I drink hot cocoa
Then do the hoco moco
The snow falls
Just as winter calls

No leaves on the tree bow
How come there's no snow now?
At last, the snow has come
Everyone's happy, except my mum!

Una McCoy (10)
St Mary's Primary School, Draperstown

Monsters

Monsters are scary and can give you a fright,
They are under your bed and creep out at night.
They've big, red eyes that glow like fire,
If you weren't scared, I'd call you a liar.
Monsters are scary and really yucky,
If you haven't seen one, I'd call you lucky.
But don't be afraid or scared to go out,
Just run like mad if you see one about!

Dearbhla McCallion (8)
St Mary's Primary School, Draperstown

The Best Winter

Winter is fun
In winter it is snowy
Now the snow starts
The snow is classic
Every winter there is snow
In the class one day, there was snow
Winter is class
Oh, how winter is a cold season!
A snowball is made of snow
The snow is classic
Right now, the snow is going away for the year.

Dara Carlin (10)
St Mary's Primary School, Draperstown

Autumn

He blows his icy breath through the cold night,
Makes the birds shiver and fly away,
Then he changes his attitude,
He takes away the old leaves,
Makes life easier for the trees,
He sometimes turns up the heat,
Only when he's in a good mood,
But when he isn't,
He turns bitter.

Michael Donnelly (11)
St Mary's Primary School, Draperstown

Colorado

My name is Ben and I've been away,
To the grand, old U S of A,

I saw the sun and lots of snow,
Off to ski, I did go,

Up the lifts, higher and higher,
Then down the slopes, a bit of a flier,

It was great to relax at the hot springs,
Good for our tired muscles and things,

If you get a chance, don't think twice,
Go to Colorado and grab a big slice *(pizza)*.

Ben McCloskey (8)
St Mary's Primary School, Draperstown

All About Winter

Winter is snowy and very blowy
It is fun for everyone
There is no sun, so come and join the fun
Winter is too cool for school
You can throw snowballs at your friends
When they are playing with their hens
After they put them in their pens
Your friends can play in the hay.

Conor Dorrity (10)
St Mary's Primary School, Draperstown

Fireworks

Big bangs these beautiful things make
Person to person
We all know some harm can come
Sometimes this thing screeches
Sometimes it can be a dud
It could be a lady getting up to dance
Or maybe a boisterous boy showing off
But when it's nearly finished
It's starting to die
When it is down
We all know it's dead
So we light another one instead.

Gemma Bradley (11)
St Mary's Primary School, Draperstown

James And The Giant Peach

G ood thing to eat
I t is healthy
A good thing to eat
N ever to be sold
T he giant peach

P lease do not sell
E at for supper
A mazing
C runchy
H alf each? No!

Meghan McGillian (8)
St Mary's Primary School, Draperstown

Football Crazy

I'm football crazy
I'm football mad
Every single evening
I play it with my dad.

When my homework's finished
He takes me to the park
Where we practise shooting
Until it's getting dark.

So, when I get older
I'll play for Liverpool
Like Stevie G or Torres
Now, won't that be cool!

Jon Paul Devlin (8)
St Mary's Primary School, Draperstown

Winter

It's like a winter wonderland,
I really do think it's grand.

The snow falls,
As winter calls.

And with all the snowball fights,
We need to turn on the Christmas lights.

Aine Michelle Lagan (10)
St Mary's Primary School, Draperstown

The Peach

Peaces are small
Peaches are big
Peaches are red and orange
What a beautiful peach to eat!

Rory McGuigan (8)
St Mary's Primary School, Draperstown

The Firework!

Fireworks all colourful and bright,
Getting ready to be set alight.

Then, they go off with a bang
And join their gang.

Then off they all fly
And brighten up the sky.

Their colours so bright,
Light up the night.

Oh, what a beautiful sight,
Disappearing into the night.

Cathy McKenna (11)
St Mary's Primary School, Draperstown

My Cat

I have a cat called Mitzy,
His fur is all fluffy and glitzy,
He runs around the house,
Chasing after a mouse,
Then eats it when its all nice and crispy!

Aaron McCloskey (8)
St Mary's Primary School, Draperstown

The Giant Peach

The giant peach is peachy
It has sweet, orange juice
It has smooth red skin
And a sweet juicy taste
The giant peach tastes so sweet and delicious.

Carla McGuigan (7)
St Mary's Primary School, Draperstown

Catherine Wheel

She's ready to sparkle,
She's ready to glow
And when she sets off
Everyone will know.

She's very beautiful
And wonderful too,
She will light up,
Just for you.

Ellen Kelly (11)
St Mary's Primary School, Draperstown

Cowgirls

Cowgirls are cool!
They wear cowboy boots
And patterned trousers like a cow
Cowgirls live in the Wild West
They ride horses and chase cows too!
Cowgirls wear hats and tie their hair in plaits
I just love cowgirls - *yeehaa!*

Aine Gray (8)
St Mary's Primary School, Draperstown

The Tall Man

There once was a man who was tall
But his ears were incredibly small
Everyone shouted, but he just pouted
Because he couldn't hear them at all!

Cara McGoldrick (8)
St Mary's Primary School, Draperstown

Autumn

What an appearance colouring the leaves
Blowing away the old ones, giving trees a break

Everyone's happy too
And there's lots of different things to do

Until the windy breeze
Boom, bang, bash, crash
See the trees making a bash

Now that it's good
Now that it's fine
Now the weather can be all mine

Now that there's no racket
You can enjoy the rest of the day

Hooray!
Let's go and play!

Dermot Hegarty (10)
St Mary's Primary School, Draperstown

Sparkly Fireworks!

I am a firework, colourful and bright,
You will see me on Hallowe'en night,
When you light me, I will screech,
You might even hear me on a beach,
When I explode you will see my true colour,
But all the others are much duller,
I'll go *bang*, you will see,
But that's the last you'll hear of me.

Annie McEldowney (10)
St Mary's Primary School, Draperstown

Fireworks Go Bang!

There is a thing that goes bang,
It can easily scare you stiff,
It can always be fun,
But sometimes you will run.
It could scare you out of your slippers
And get you running in some flippers.
Then you will be glad,
Then you'll have to run like mad,
So it would be good if you stay away,
Or else you will be blown all away!

Thomas Gillespie (11)
St Mary's Primary School, Draperstown

Fireworks!

Colourful and bright
Lights up the night
He is very beautiful
And very wonderful
He likes to show off his spark
When it's very, very dark
Then he is above your head
But before you know it - he is dead.

Rachel Kelly (11)
St Mary's Primary School, Draperstown

Autumn!

Autumn is cool, but not always,
It can be a bit angry or shivery.
One autumn day, I went out to play,
But I was so cold I had to come in.
Mum,
Why is the wind blowing with fear?
Why is the wind calling my name?
The wind is fierce and very cool,
But I don't think the trees like him,
Because he is a fool.
The leaves fall off
And the trees shiver,
Please stop being bad,
Because I don't like it.

Caroline Rafferty (10)
St Mary's Primary School, Draperstown

Fireworks

Colourful and bright
As it lights up the night
Like a performer in the dark
As it shows off its spark
It's such a fantastic sight
As its set alight,
It shoots up with a scream,
If its works like a dream
And then suddenly you're in a hospital bed
With burns on your head.

Cahir McEldowney (11)
St Mary's Primary School, Draperstown

Starburst!

Starburst, hopped into my life
I couldn't even sleep right that night
All I could think of was her long, floppy ears
And bright, marble eyes
I was so excited
She was such a surprise
She ate, twitched and nibbled on sticks
And then I was wondering
What she would do next
Starburst, I gave her that name
She burst into my life
And it will never be the same.

Fionnuala Hegarty (11)
St Mary's Primary School, Draperstown

Fireworks

A firework is a show off
Who tries to give a show

So he lights up the night, good and bright
As he explodes with a wonderful glow

For he is the one who makes a giant spark
As he sets off in the dark

Colourful and bright, turning the night
Into the most wonderful, colourful show!

Stephen Halferty (11)
St Mary's Primary School, Draperstown

The Magical Adventure

So, the mighty, golden, full-sailed ship
Set off through a milk chocolate sea.
The king saw wondrous sights,
From fluffy fish to ice cream trees . . .
Through a rainbow whirlpool
And on around a bend.
Until he was in Topsy-Turvy-dom
His travels were at an end!

The king saw mixed-up bodies
Like a zebra and a giraffe
And a baby going to work
And even one on a raft!
Birds in the sea
And fish in the air
And humans that were hairy
And rabbits that were bare!

The king took a dive in the sea
And swam beside the birds.
Then he climbed up to the top of the island
And played with walking and talking words!
He rook a ride with the fish in the air
And got aboard a train.
He also bounced in the clouds
And played in the rain!

The king returned to his big, mighty ship
And said goodbye to his friends.
So, he set out into the milk chocolate sea
And back around the bends.
When he got back to Quizzical Island,
He went to see the queen.
Then they both sat down to a dinner,
Of potatoes, carrots and beans.

Damien McCoy (8)
St Mary's Primary School, Draperstown

The Volcano

The volcano was a mean man
His voice was a roaring thunder

As his lava rushed down
Fast and furious

When the volcano sees something
They turn to stone as they try to hide

He tries so hard to find
As he squeezes through the tunnel

His red hair boiling up and down
Eventually, he goes to sleep

The burned-up city
Still has some people.

Clare Cuskeran (10)
St Mary's Primary School, Draperstown

My Birthday

Today's the day, it's finally here,
It's my birthday, give me a cheer,
Friends on the way, they'll be here all day,
Let's have some fun, that's what I say,
Got loads of presents, got loads of food,
Everyone's here, let's get in the mood,
Friends make me laugh, friends make me cry,
Wasn't much cake, but no one asked why,
All of a sudden, Shaun started humming,
He won't tell me why, next year he's not coming!

Adam Harlow (11)
St Mary's Primary School, Draperstown

Mr Autumn

This is the time of year we say
That Mr Autumn is on his way.

He paints the leaves on the trees
Then he helps grow the peas.

He lets the trees have a rest
So, now they think he's the best.

He helps plants disperse their seeds
And now he does some good deeds.

So, he is away now, my friends
Until next year, that's his end.

Ciaran Breen (10)
St Mary's Primary School, Draperstown

The Beach

I love going to the beach,
On a sunbathing summer's day.
I love being with my family
And to swim and play and play!

I love to build sandcastles
And to have a tennis match.
I love to collect shells that dazzle
And then settle down with the tide and watch.

I love the beach! I adore it!
Next time I go, I must thank it!

Elena Torres (11)
St Michael's Primary School, Belfast

Snowy Day

I looked outside on that cold winter's day
And saw snow lying out evenly on the once green grass.
I put on my coat and boots and ran outside to play.
I had a snowball fight with my younger sister.
Then I had a clever idea to build a snowman.
Some time later my mum called me in.
I looked out on the snow thinking,
This snow was once crisp and even.
The next day I looked outside
Hopeful to find that the snow had melted away.

Clodagh Smith (11)
St Michael's Primary School, Belfast

Recipe For A Weekend

An ounce of sleeping in
A kilogram of football
Beat some PlayStation and TV
Until it is like dough
Whip up some basketball and hurling
Whip for about five minutes until it is creamy.

When you have done that
Sprinkle a bit of fighting with your big brother
And playing with your friends.

Niall Smyth (10)
St Michael's Primary School, Belfast

They're Going To Break My Glasses

There are monsters in my bed with me
And they're trying to wrestle with me
And they're going to break my glasses!

One is fat and one is lean.
One is small and one is big.
One has big eyes, one is bad,
One has sharp teeth and claws
And one is hairy.
One is floppy and one has big feet.
One is purple and one is green
And they're going to break my glasses!

I've got them where I want them
And they're small again.
They're going to bed
And they haven't broken my glasses.

Dermot O'Hare (11)
St Michael's Primary School, Belfast

Happiness

Happiness sounds like laughter from children.
It tastes as sweet as a candy apple.
It smells like daisies in a field.
It looks like a kitten playing with string.
It feels like puppies' fur.
It reminds me of a rabbit hopping through a field.

Joanne Madden-McKee (10)
St Michael's Primary School, Belfast

In The Morning

In the morning, my alarm goes off
So, yawning I get out of bed.
I stumble to find the wardrobe
And end up in the shed! Huh?

OK, so I'm half asleep,
It's like this you see.
I was meant to go to bed at nine
And went at half-past three! Oops!

I finally get my uniform on,
I'm running really late.
I waffle some toast and grab a bag,
Full of Dad's fishing bait! Yuck!

I run back in and grab my bag,
I made sure of that
And I noticed when I got to class
It had been puked on by the cat! *Eewh*!

Niamh Kelly (10)
St Michael's Primary School, Belfast

Darkness

Darkness tastes like food
that has grown old and stale.
It smells like the dankness, gloominess
and sadness of a graveyard.
It looks like a thick black enshrouding blanket
of sadness and misery.
It feels like a net trapping you in it.
It reminds me of fog which slowly creeps into everything.

Jacob Meehan (11)
St Michael's Primary School, Belfast

Haze

He was standing there.
Just standing looking at something.
I don't know what it was.
He was just standing blankly.
Somebody saw the same thing.
Ask them.

It was weird.
Everything was cold and this was no light breeze.
A cloud of smoke appeared at the door.
At least I think it was smoke.
I heard something.
A black shadow appeared at the roof.
Everything went silent and there was a beam of light.
That's all I remember. That house.

Nicholas Kearney (10)
St Michael's Primary School, Belfast

Fear

Fear sounds like a scream in the distance.
Fear tastes like a sour lemon in your mouth.
Fear smells like a dark, dirty alley.
Fear looks like a white face, cold and frozen.
Fear feels like cold water dripping down your spine.
Fear reminds me of ice being scraped at with a sharp blade.

Becky Guirova (11)
St Michael's Primary School, Belfast

School

S chool is boring with nothing to do
   but listen to teachers talk and talk.
C hildren at school do millions of subjects
   and hardly get a break for a walk
H eadmasters and mistresses are the worst
   they make you look perfect and smart
O f course there are some very rare subjects I like
   such as PE, ICT and art
O nly twice in school do you get a break
   and can chat with a friend
L ast subject at school is maths but no one listens
   because they are all waiting for school to *end*.

Niamh Healy (10)
St Michael's Primary School, Belfast

Happiness

Happiness sounds like people having fun.
Happiness tastes like hot chocolate with melted marshmallows.
Happiness smells like melted chocolate.
Happiness looks like home with your family in front of a cosy fire.
Happiness feels like when someone hugs you.
Happiness reminds me of playing with my best friends.
That's what happiness is!

Catherine Kilgallen (11)
St Michael's Primary School, Belfast

Snow

I'm waking up in a cosy bed,
I look out the window and see a winter wonderland for miles.
My heart jumps for joy at the sight of this deserted wilderness
                                                      of white snow.

I pull on my insulated clothes faster than ever before.
I get the keys and open the stiff cold door
And here I am in the middle of this tranquil white world.

Crunch, crunch as I go,
Breaking up this blanket of snow,
Fluffy, soft, light and elegant it feels,
Crunchy, I'm submerged in snow.

Ben O'Kane (8)
St Michael's Primary School, Belfast

Anger

Anger sounds like a bomb exploding on the ground.
Anger tastes like a sour lemon squeezing through your throat.
Anger smells like a stink bomb rushing through the air
And landing with a putrid smell.
It looks like little children vomiting up last night's Brussels sprouts.
It feels like a boiling hot chilli bubbling up inside your stomach.
Anger reminds me of a boxing match
And the hatred the two boxers have for each other.

Cormac Meehan (11)
St Michael's Primary School, Belfast

A Snowflake

There is a snowflake in the air,
Big, beautiful, it is one that is rare.
It looks like a circle of silk,
It is as white as milk.
It is as smooth as leather
And it is as light as a feather.
There is a blanket of white on the ground,
It is as fluffy as cirrus clouds.
It gleams like shining stars
And it looks beautiful on silver cars.

Fiona Currie (8)
St Michael's Primary School, Belfast

Autumn

Autumn is here
And Hallowe'en is near.
The leaves are falling
And the wind is calling.
The rain is pouring really heavy
And now I'm stuck in bed with teddy.
Leaves are gold, orange, yellow and brown,
They flutter and dance all through town.

Amy Gogarty (9)
St Michael's Primary School, Belfast

A Snowflake

When snowflakes fall,
It's so amazing,
Tucked up in bed,
The fire is blazing!
Look outside,
There's plenty to see,
When snowflakes fall,
They look so free!
When snowflakes fall,
They look so white,
But if you stay too long,
You'll get frostbite!
But as winter ends,
The snow descends,
But we had fun,
As it sparkled in the sun!

Tom McVeigh (9)
St Michael's Primary School, Belfast

Darkness

Darkness tastes like old milk
as putrid as can be.
It smells like a demon
who hasn't washed in years.
Darkness looks like two eyes
staring straight at you.
It feels big and hairy
like it's going to eat you
and last of all it reminds me
of a black dove.

Brandon Daly (11)
St Michael's Primary School, Belfast

A Snowflake

Hi! Look at me
I'm the one you can feel and see
I gently fall from the sky
And land softly on the ground
On your hair and everywhere
I'm not that small, I'm beautiful
I'm as white as crystal, I'm glittering
I make a blanket of snow
Soon it will turn into a winter wonderland
After sunrise I'll vanish instantly!

Aobh Hughes (8)
St Michael's Primary School, Belfast

Snowflake

A snowflake is very small.
You can join them to make a ball.
One that you can throw,
So people will fall in the snow.

Children enjoy going out to play in the snow.
It makes their faces glow.
People enjoy skating on the ice.
When they fall it is not very nice.

Daire Magee (8)
St Michael's Primary School, Belfast

Autumn Is Here

All the leaves are falling.
They have changed colour
From green to amber, gold and brown
They whirl and twirl in the wind
The weather is getting colder
As the days are getting shorter
And the nights are longer
Squirrels are busy getting ready for winter
Hallowe'en is close by
When children go trick or treating
And fireworks fly.

Declan McCartney (9)
St Michael's Primary School, Belfast

A Poem Of Sport

It feels fun to play,
Giving you the adrenaline rush of shooting a gun,
But when the other team has won,
It looks like a rubber gun,
But everyone has won because every point is a pin
And every win is just a pin in an empty bin
And at the end there is always a grin on a chin!

Dáire Cumiskey (10)
St Michael's Primary School, Belfast

My Family

My brother is a brat, there's no doubt about that.
My mum is very nice and she buys me lots of sweets.
My dad is very artistic and taught me how to paint
And to me he is a saint.
My dog Tara is even better than me,
She snuggles down beside me and starts licking me.
But last but not least there's me.

Sean McGrillen (11)
St Michael's Primary School, Belfast

Snowflakes

Snowflakes are made of icy water.
They flutter around the street and make a blanket of white.
They're cold to the body but a joy to the eye.
Each snowflake is unique
And together they make a perfect tool for winter games.
Snowball fights and snowmen are such a wonderful sight.
Gradually, when the sun comes out they silently melt away.

Alex Symes (9)
St Michael's Primary School, Belfast

Autumn

Autumn is here,
The leaves are falling off the tree, gold, orange and brown.
The frost is crisp and clear,
In the early morning the spiders' webs are glistening.
The squirrels are filling their dreys with acorns and nuts
While the birds are flying south for winter.
Now autumn has ended, all the animals have hibernated.

Jake Carlin (9)
St Michael's Primary School, Belfast

Fun

Fun sounds like lots of kids playing together.
It tastes like a slice of chocolate cake
And also it smells like hot chocolate.
It looks like snowball fights in the winter
And it feels like being kind to old people and sharing.
It reminds me of playing a game of cards with my dad.

Francesca McVey (11)
St Michael's Primary School, Belfast

A Snowflake

A snowflake is as light as a feather
It looks like a piece of white leather
It is very clear like a crystal
They come in all shapes and sizes
When they fall down from the sky it's a beautiful sight
The snowflakes fall on top of one another
They make a blanket of white wilderness
The sun comes out and melts the snow
Bye-bye snow, see you later.

Timothy Cunningham (8)
St Michael's Primary School, Belfast

Snowflakes

Snowflakes are white as fluffy clouds.
They're smooth as pebble and clear as crystal.
As they fall on the ground they form a blanket of snow.
They come in all different, beautiful designs.
They are icy and pure as Jack Frost.
They are smooth and silky.
Millions of snowflakes make a frosty winter wonderland.

Olivia Ray (9)
St Michael's Primary School, Belfast

A Snowflake

A snowflake is cold and white
They come in different designs
Some are big, others are small
No two snowflakes in the world are the same
They are pure, clean and beautiful
They look smooth to touch
As the sun comes out the snowflake will drift away.

Tara Faulkner (9)
St Michael's Primary School, Belfast

Autumn

Autumn has come.
The oak, sycamore and beech trees are swaying from side to side.
The red, gold and amber leaves twirl like Irish dancers.
The swallows are flying south to warmer countries
And the native red squirrels are collecting nuts.
The days are full of mist, fog and sometimes it's raining cats
                                                     and dogs.
The bushes are glistening with spiders' webs all over them.
Conkers are falling off the horse chestnut trees.
Autumn is such a colourful time of year.

Andy Harney (8)
St Michael's Primary School, Belfast

A Snowflake

The snowflakes are falling everywhere
Some are landing gracefully on my skin.
I love the gentle drops of wet on my face.
The snowman is as wet as a beautiful white fluffy cloud.
Each one has six sides
And is shaped like a crystal.
They come in many beautiful designs.
Now that it is melting there is no more snow to play with anymore.

Tony Crawford (9)
St Michael's Primary School, Belfast

The Autumn Dance

Leaves turn crimson, scarlet, amber, brown and yellow
Then the north wind blows and the leaves begin to dance
Arm in arm they begin to whirl, twirl, spin and twist
Then sway back and forth to the music of the howling wind
Then when their dance is finished and when the music stops
They flutter to the ground and make a beautiful patch blanket
And rest snugly on the ground.

Keela McConville (9)
St Michael's Primary School, Belfast

Autumn Is Here

Autumn is here.
The leaves are falling off the trees like colourful bits of dust,
Amber, scarlet, gold, red and rust.
They flutter down to make a warm quilt on the ground.

The frost is coming.
The skies are often dark and grey.
The squirrels are collecting acorns to fill their dreys.
There is nothing like autumn when it's here!

Hannah Griffin (9)
St Michael's Primary School, Belfast

A Snowflake

Snow is falling everywhere
Oh what a beautiful sight
Snowmen will soon be about
Snowflakes are dancing from up above
Coming in all different shapes and sizes and beautiful designs
More snowflakes are flying like lots of butterflies
Together they make a white wilderness of fun
Snowflakes falling down to make a winter wonderland!

Laura Jane Quinn (8)
St Michael's Primary School, Belfast

A Snowflake

I fall gently from the sky with my comrades floating by.
I am white and small, you can make me into a ball.
Look at me but don't touch me because I am as delicate as a filigree.
Soon I will fall into a submerged wilderness of white.

Lorcan Fahy (8)
St Michael's Primary School, Belfast

The Magic Box
(Inspired by 'Magic Box' by Kit Wright)

In my magic box are all my hopes and dreams.
And all my sweetest smells.
All my dreams fly out of the magic box
And come true.
I hope that a black rabbit flies out of my box.
I close it and hide it.

Ciara O'Doherty (8)
St Paul's Primary School, Londonderry

Spies

Spies, spies they can do anything
They can even track down a dragon that flies.
Spies are sneaking along the floor
And they can dodge a trap door.
Spies so crafty climbing walls,
They can even jump over a mountain of balls.

Reece Ogle (9)
St Paul's Primary School, Londonderry

Dreams

D reams' themes they are all great,
R hyming rhymes all the time,
E arth is where we live together,
A mazing adventures all the time,
M agic fairies all at night,
S uper dreams all day and night.

Bradley Belgrave (8)
St Paul's Primary School, Londonderry

Happiness

H appiness is great.
A happy day.
P eople happy all the time
P eople laughing.
I love my mum and dad.
N ever let love stop.
E veryone happy
S chool make me happy.
S hare happiness.

Caitlin Goodfellow (8)
St Paul's Primary School, Londonderry

Football

F ootball is excellent
O utside playing every day
O ften in the rain
T he world is peaceful
B eing manager is good
A lso being the boss
L iverpool is the best team
L ovely football.

Sean Burke
St Paul's Primary School, Londonderry

Night

N ight there is nothing in sight
I n the night bats are about
G azing at nothing
H earing nothing but bats
T he night is so dark you need a light.

Tony Whoriskey (8)
St Paul's Primary School, Londonderry

Spies

Spies, spies everywhere.
Spies all around the world,
In Galway and America.
Hiding in shadows and the alleys.
Spies, spies watching us right now.
Cameras all around us.
From hideouts in the shadows.

Watching you.

Feargal Mellon
St Paul's Primary School, Londonderry

Football

F ootball is good
O ften we play it
O utside playing it all day
T he teams are good and football is fun
B eing the captain is fun
A rsenal is the team I am
L iverpool is the team I'm playing
L iverpool and Arsenal both drew.

Christopher McQuaid (8)
St Paul's Primary School, Londonderry

Dreams

D reams are everywhere
R eading books make them anywhere
E very time you get them when you sleep
A ll the time when you're sleeping
M ountains, castles, even fairies
S weet dreams every time.

Shay Cavanagh (8)
St Paul's Primary School, Londonderry

Memories

One,
    My first tooth came.
Two,
    Giving up my bottle and dummy.
Three,
    When I walked to the shop and got knocked down.
Four,
    I first started school.
Five,
    Playing with my new friends.
Six,
    Playing in the garden with my little sister.
Seven,
    Inviting my friends to my birthday.
Eight,
    Going to Red Castle with my teacher.
Nine,
    I went up the town with my mummy to spend my birthday money.
Ten,
    I got a ring and a new outfit and lots of money for my birthday.

Samantha Boyle (11)
St Paul's Primary School, Londonderry

Keeping My Own Company

I play football in the big field, I practise shots.
I jog around the back square 10 times.
I go out to my back garden and draw some birds sitting in the trees.
I go to the beach for a swim.
I listen to my favourite CDs up in my bedroom.

Odhran Scarlett (10)
St Paul's Primary School, Londonderry

Whatif?
(Based on 'Whatif' by Shel Silverstein)

Last night while I lay thinking here
Some 'whatifs' crawled inside my ear
And pranced and parties all night long
And sang their same old 'whatif' song:
Whatif my friends hate me?
Whatif I lose my money?
Whatif I fall out of my top bunk?
Whatif my window gets smashed?
Whatif I drown when swimming?
Whatif I get cancer?
Whatif an alien chases me?
Whatif a dog attacks me?
Whatif I forget my PE gear?
Whatif I get lots of homework?
Whatif I get killed?
Whatif my pet runs away?
Whatif I move school?
Whatif I move house?
Everything seems swell
And then the night-time 'whatifs' strike again.

Bronagh Robinson (10)
St Paul's Primary School, Londonderry

I Saw A Peacock

I saw a peacock with good shoes,
I saw a man with lots of fur,
I saw a dog cook dinner,
I saw my mum paint a tree,
I saw an artist fly in the sky,
I saw a bird wearing gloves,
I saw a boy suck a baby bottle,
I saw a baby far away from home,
I saw a woman who saw these too
And said though strange all were true.

Gary James Burke (10)
St Paul's Primary School, Londonderry

In The Dark!

While I was sleeping last night I woke,
I thought I heard someone who spoke.
Who could it have been?
Guess what I have seen?
Nothing,
Not a thing.
I was real scared,
I pretended I didn't care.
I looked at the window,
There was a shadow.
Then I heard a *rustle* in the bushes,
Was it *monsters* making fusses?
I hid under my duvet,
Maybe it was a *zombie*?
Could it be a *skeleton*?
Then I heard a bell, *ding dong*.
I was so scared I nearly jumped out of my skin,
I saw a black figure which was thin.
Then came footsteps on the stairs,
I was nearly in tears!

Shauneen Cavanagh (10)
St Paul's Primary School, Londonderry

In The Dark

As I lie in bed my liver does shiver
I scream but I do like ice cream
When I go to bed I hear the wind and scream
I hear the wind going with the zombies
I hate the wind, it makes me scared
I dream of zombies dreaming of me
And staring at me
The ghosts are up in my ceiling
And all the blinds are closed
I am scared
I hate creepy crawlies.

Priscilla Corcoran (9)
St Paul's Primary School, Londonderry

In A Girl's Head

In my head I dream my friends are lost.
I love to eat pizza on a Saturday night.
The game I like to play is hide-and-seek.
School is good when we do good things.
I don't like big, long and hard homework.
I dream about loads of clothes in my house.
In my dream I always dream about my favourite TV programme
And I dream about me selling DVDs.
I love to get music all the time.
I dream about new things coming into our town.
I saw a lovely dog in my dream.
I love to read loads of books.
There is much promise in the circumstance
That so many people have heads.

Chloé McClintock (10)
St Paul's Primary School, Londonderry

A Boy's Head

My friends play football with me.
They are the best.
I think of watching Manchester United play.
My favourite game is FIFA '08.
My favourite programme is The Simpsons.
I am thinking of playing for Manchester United.
My dog is very playful.
My favourite food is burger and chips.
I like hearing ghost stories.
I think of a lot of things, but it is good to see things inside
                                                  of your head.
In the circumstances that so many people have a good mind.

Jamie Dunne (10)
St Paul's Primary School, Londonderry

In The Dark

A man ran across the attic
While I was lying in my bed,
Someone rustled the trees,
I thought it was a bat.

I was so scared,
I heard a scary noise,
I thought it was a monster,
But it was a witch.

I saw an eagle flying
And a freaky shadow,
The floorboards were squeaking,
I heard a loud scream.

I was so afraid,
So I ran into my mum's room
And she said, 'What's that matter?'
And I said, 'I just had a nightmare.'

Demilee Collett (10)
St Paul's Primary School, Londonderry

Family

F un with my family
A happy family
M um is there for me all the time
I n the house I have fun with my family
L ots of people in my family
Y oung baby in my family.

Reece O'Kane (8)
St Paul's Primary School, Londonderry

In The Dark

In the dark I am scared
Soon the shadows come alive
Then the door starts to creak
And the wind pushes at the door

In the dark outside my room
I see a ghost looking at me
He is tall and black and has dark eyes

I look out the window and what do I see?
A man that looks like scream
He makes me jump out of bed
And he is freaky

He is tall and black
With long arms as big as me
And makes the room as cold as ice.

Caolán Ramsay (10)
St Paul's Primary School, Londonderry

A Girl's Head

I imagine
My sixteenth birthday,
A large chocolate cake saying my name on it
And in the goody bags a diamond ring.
Still thinking of the time when
My granny's dog bit me.
In my head I see
Man-U beating Arsenal 5-0 *goal* . . .
I imagine me
On a holiday to Barbados,
Living like a celebrity
And thinking of chocolate
And strawberries.
There is much promise
In that circumstance
That so, many people have heads.

Saoirse McCormick (10)
St Paul's Primary School, Londonderry

In The Dark

While I'm lying in my bed, cold and scared,
Sounds from the street can be heard.
Hearing sounds which are freaky
And the floorboards which are creaky.

Watching out for monsters here and there,
Now I see zombies coming everywhere.
Hearing screams from here and there,
Knowing ghosts will give me a scare.

Shivering cold in my bed,
Seeing a shadowy head.
Silent now so I hear,
But the dark still gives me fear.

Seeing a scary face on the wall,
That is what scares me most of all.
Squeaks coming from the floor,
Now I hear them no more.

Aaron Dalzell (10)
St Paul's Primary School, Londonderry

Ginger Cat Limerick

There once was a ginger cat
Who was so very fat
She fell down the stairs
And into some chairs
And that was the end of that.

Shannon Gaw (9)
Woodlawn Primary School, Carrickfergus

Happy Valentine's!

Happy I am with you
As day by day you are more pretty
People like you would be sweet
People should be more like you
You make me happy
Valentine's makes me happy
As you grow you are more beautiful
Let me look at you every day
Every day you are so pretty
Never in my life I have seen someone prettier
To my heart you are my valentine
I will never let you out of my heart
Never in my life you were prettier
Ever in my life you are prettier
So can you be my valentine?

Victoria Shearer (10)
Woodlawn Primary School, Carrickfergus

Meg's Limerick

There once was a girl called Meg
Who always ate raw eggs
She told her mummy
'Cause she had a sore tummy
So she had to stay in bed.

Courtney Best (9)
Woodlawn Primary School, Carrickfergus

Snake Limerick

There once was a very long snake
Who really loved to bake cakes
He had some fun
While making some buns
And his tummy started to ache.

Rebekah Stewart (8)
Woodlawn Primary School, Carrickfergus

Happy Valentine's

Happy Valentine's Day
As you are so sweet
People like you as a treat
People should be more like you
You are the one I like
Valentine, you always have a smile on your face
As I like you very much
Love is in the air
Even though there are more people in the world
No one can take your place
To you I give this with hugs and kisses
In my heart you are my star
Never will you not be my valentine
Eyes they are so sweet
So . . . will you be my valentine?

Erin McAllister (10)
Woodlawn Primary School, Carrickfergus

Babby-Rib

Babby doesn't chew his food
His mum and dad say it's rude,
But Babby-Rib doesn't care
He just says, *'It's not fair!'*
One day his aunt came to town
And his mum and dad said, 'Don't let us down.'
'I'll be good, I'll be good,
I promise I will chew my food.'
Two days later his aunt came to town,
But all she could give him was a frown,
You see, his aunt was very strict
And every time he sees her, Babby will be sick!

Leah Thompson (10)
Woodlawn Primary School, Carrickfergus

Babby-Rib

Babby doesn't chew his food,
His mum and dad says it's rude,
But Babby-Rib doesn't care,
He just says, 'It's not fair!'
One day his aunt came to town
And his mum and dad said, 'Don't let us down.'
'I'll be good, I'll be good,
I promise I will chew my food.'
Two days later his aunt came to town,
But all she could give him was a frown,
You see, his aunt was very strict
And every time he sees her,
Babby will be sick!

Simon Scott (10)
Woodlawn Primary School, Carrickfergus

Love Is All Around

Love is all around
In my heart and all around
Very deep down in the pit of my heart
Everywhere I go
Round and round, love is near
Present, what you bring
Over and over
Over and over
Love is all around.

Jamie Karl Wallace (10)
Woodlawn Primary School, Carrickfergus

Friends

Friends are the ones who follow you,
Wherever you may go,
Whenever you think you're all alone they'll smile and say hello.
When you're in the maths class
And you don't know what to do,
They'll tap you on the shoulder and say,
'Try multiply by two!'
When you're in the playground
And you fall and hurt your knee,
They will put their hand up,
'My friend has fallen Miss, you see?'
Friends are always there for you
And help with what you do,
So give them kindness in return
And they'll be kind to you!

Emma Baird (10)
Woodlawn Primary School, Carrickfergus

You're My Valentine

I love you so much,
Wherever you are
You're always shining,
As bright as a star,
You're always so sweet
When I kiss you on the cheek.

Chloe Greenaway (10)
Woodlawn Primary School, Carrickfergus

Happiness

Happiness is in my heart,
Happiness is in my heart wherever I may go,
All my happiness is not able to come out.
Pumping my blood through my veins by happiness,
Possibly I get my happiness from deep down inside my heart.
Inside my heart feels like I'm going to explode with joy,
Now this is not a piece of work.
Enjoyment is what I do this for, not for anything else,
So now it's just the time to say that I feel happy in every way.
Soon I will be older and it will still matter to me,
'Cause I still want to be that little girl who was always happy.

Caitlin Eve Robin (9)
Woodlawn Primary School, Carrickfergus

The World Around Me

The world around me
Is fresh and green,
The loveliest sight
You've ever seen,
The flowers are pretty,
The sky is blue,
Then oh!
I hear the cows go moo!

Ashleigh Milliken (9)
Woodlawn Primary School, Carrickfergus

Watching The Sunset

You're as cuddly
As a teddy bear,
And if I was one
You would always care.
When I take a seat
You're always so neat,
When we're watching the sunset . . .

Demi Davies (10)
Woodlawn Primary School, Carrickfergus

Mouse

A fur lump
A fast crawler
A silent creeper
A currant dropper
A cheese nibbler
A small squeak
A wood nibbler
A cat's feast.

Hannah Barbour (10)
Woodlawn Primary School, Carrickfergus

Scared

The cat leaves the tower in fear
but no one else is near.
He is walking down the street
not aware there's not a peep.

Sophie Duff (10)
Woodlawn Primary School, Carrickfergus

My Dog Bill

My name's Phil,
I've got a dog called Bill,
He's very flirty,
But also very dirty.
He sleeps in a bed
With a spider web,
Have you see Bill?
Oh my name's Phill.

Abigail Kerr (10)
Woodlawn Primary School, Carrickfergus

Loneliness

My heart not beating,
I'm lost in a dark forest,
No one beside me,
Everywhere a dark mist hangs,
The windows are painted black.

Sophie Irwin (11)
Woodlawn Primary School, Carrickfergus

The Cat And The Rats

The cat leaves the tower in fear
Because the rats are coming near
Through the window, up the wall
To an old church hall
Now she's never away from home.

Abby Nicholl (10)
Woodlawn Primary School, Carrickfergus

A Snake

A sly slither,
A poisonous hisser,
A mice muncher,
An egg layer,
Beady eyed,
A forked tongue
And scaly skin.

Chloe Mitchell (11)
Woodlawn Primary School, Carrickfergus

Lonely

I talk to my doll,
Wish with all my heart and strength,
That someone would come,
I shout, but get no reply,
The world has gone and left me.

Nicole Magill (10)
Woodlawn Primary School, Carrickfergus

Lonely

No one to play with
The whole wide world ignores me
Nobody wants me
No one thinks I exist
I'm like a forgotten toy.

Ben Grange (11)
Woodlawn Primary School, Carrickfergus

Loneliness

Darkness upon me
Nobody to talk to me
Nothing exciting
I'm lost in a lonely world
Stepping into a black hole.

Lee Beattie (11)
Woodlawn Primary School, Carrickfergus

Happiness

My face is shining,
I am full of happiness,
I have no worries,
I am completely carefree,
My great life is filled with joy.

Ryan Dillon (11)
Woodlawn Primary School, Carrickfergus

Darkness

Shadowing darkness,
Falling into a dark hole,
Left to go alone,
Loneliness is a dark room,
Where you can never get out.

Jordan Bell (11)
Woodlawn Primary School, Carrickfergus

Kitten

A soundless sleeper,
A vibrating purr,
A trouble maker,
A sneaky pouncer,
A sharp scratcher,
A milk slurper,
A ham nibbler,
A fur ball.

Emily Brownlee (11)
Woodlawn Primary School, Carrickfergus

Sadness Has Arrived

My tears now dripping,
A huge, big puddle I make.
My background is blue,
I wish I could have some fun,
But I feel like I'm left out.

Rachel Close (11)
Woodlawn Primary School, Carrickfergus

Dog

A cuddly toy,
A greedy eater,
A fast runner,
A hole digger,
A house polluter,
A fluffy shadow,
A sneaky listener,
A drooling machine.

Chealsea Waite (11)
Woodlawn Primary School, Carrickfergus

A Mouse

A nosy nuisance,
A mischievous listener,
A cat patroniser,
A tiny terror,
A cheese muncher,
A tailed horror,
A squeaking nibbler,
A whiskered glider.

Jake Adams (11)
Woodlawn Primary School, Carrickfergus

Teachers

Teachers are a helping hand,
When things start to get tough,
They help you when you're sad or scared,
When kids are playing rough,
They aren't just mean and bossy,
Like you hear from all your friends,
But a person who will help you
Right through until the very end.

Ellen Minford (11)
Woodlawn Primary School, Carrickfergus

Sadness

Shadows in darkness,
Hay rolling around the street,
Grey on my doorstep
Like a polluted river,
In this world I feel disowned.

Shannon Clarke (11)
Woodlawn Primary School, Carrickfergus

View Of A Polar Bear

A fluff ball,
An ice-skater,
A fluffy blanket,
A fish devourer,
A brilliant camouflage,
A horrific beast,
A lion's roar,
King of the ice.

Reece McDowell (11)
Woodlawn Primary School, Carrickfergus

A Star

One night in my garden,
I looked up in the sky and saw a star,
This one stood out like money on the ground,
It was like magic, it shone so bright,
It was so beautiful that it felt like a dream.

Jessica McCully (11)
Woodlawn Primary School, Carrickfergus

Blowing Rose - Haiku

A rose so gentle,
The petals blow in the wind
And watch the sky.

Leigh-Anne Gould (11)
Woodlawn Primary School, Carrickfergus

My Dog

A black shadow
A family protector
A fast pacer
A super sniffer
A deep growler
A ball fetcher
A cat chaser
Slobber monster!

Laura Smyth (10)
Woodlawn Primary School, Carrickfergus

Lurking Loneliness

Alone, on my own,
In my own dull and dark world,
Everywhere is spinning,
Even my own spinning head,
Loneliness is a bad curse.

Rebecca Adams (11)
Woodlawn Primary School, Carrickfergus

Loneliness

Gloomy loneliness,
follows me in a dark hole.
Wherever I go,
even when I go to eat,
loneliness lurks over me.

Reece Griffith (10)
Woodlawn Primary School, Carrickfergus

Night Noises

At night when it is dark and I am in bed
and I can't get to sleep I hear noises.
The first sound I hear is the wind.
I like to pretend it is the pixies coming,
it makes me feel happy.

Then I hear the river.
I like to pretend it is the pixies whispering to me, 'Wake up!'
It makes me feel scared.

The last sound I hear is my mum talking.
I like to pretend it is the pixies casting a spell on me.
It makes me feel confused.

In the end I wake up to find that I am a pixie.

Rebecca McIlwaine (7)
Woodlawn Primary School, Carrickfergus

Night Noises

At night when it is dark and I can't get to sleep I hear noises,
The first sound I hear is something falling,
But I like to pretend it's the night monkey falling down the stairs.

Then I hear the wind blowing
But I like to pretend it's the night monkey watching TV.

The last sound I hear is my bed squeaking,
But I like to pretend it's the night monkey climbing up the ladder.

'I'm coming!' he whispers!

Ben Crook (7)
Woodlawn Primary School, Carrickfergus

Trees

Trees sway left and right,
Don't know what to think about,
While the sun shines bright.

Amber Eyres (10)
Woodlawn Primary School, Carrickfergus

Night Noises

At night when it is dark and I am in bed
I can't get to sleep, I hear noises.
The first sound I hear is the tumble drier left on,
I pretend it's the terror ghost's belly rumbling,
It makes me feel scared
Then I hear a cat outside,
I like to pretend it's the terror ghost crying,
It makes me feel freaked out.

The last sound is the owl,
I like to pretend it is the terror ghost laughing,
It makes me feel terrified.

In the end he goes and I fall asleep.

Adam Crook (8)
Woodlawn Primary School, Carrickfergus

Night Noises

At night when it is dark and I am in bed
and I can't get to sleep I hear noises.
The first sound I hear is *squeak, squeak*.
I pretend it is the ghost opening my door.
It makes me feel scared.

Then I hear the sound of the wall tapping.
I pretend it is the ghost walking on the floor.
It makes me feel frightened.

The last sound I hear is a cat outside.
I pretend it is the ghost crying.
It makes me feel terrified.

In the end I fall asleep.

Katie Mitchell (8)
Woodlawn Primary School, Carrickfergus

Young Writers Information

We hope you have enjoyed reading this book - and that you will continue to enjoy it in the coming years.

If you like reading and writing poetry drop us a line, or give us a call, and we'll send you a free information pack.

Alternatively if you would like to order further copies of this book or any of our other titles, then please give us a call or log onto our website at www.youngwriters.co.uk

Young Writers Information
Remus House
Coltsfoot Drive
Peterborough
PE2 9JX

(01733) 890066